CLEAN UP

Wipe Your Debt Away

Learn How Starting a **Residential Cleaning Service** Can Change Your Life and Lead to **Financial Freedom**

Teresa E. Garvin

ISBN: 172318361x

ISBN-13: 978-1723183614

Dedication

I dedicate this book to everyone who has already started their own cleaning service, also to those who will take on the challenge to become independent.

I have written this book to help you to make few steps closer to your goals.

It is my dream, that this book will help at least 100 people become independent. I dedicate this book to those people.

This book contains enough information to start and run a successful business.

Please let me know if it helped you.

This book is to your success!

Supplementary Resources

I would just to say thank you for buying my book and would like to give you two PDF`s 100% FREE!

Download the PDF's: '*Magnetic Marketing 2'* - **FREE!**

'*Magnetic Marketing 2'* is also a great read for those starting out in the commercial cleaning industry.

To download go to: https://teresagarvin.com/bonus-pdf/

As a bonus: You will have access to my website where you can visit anytime when in doubt. You will be able to ask any questions related to the residential cleaning services industry that will be answered promptly.

Get this access with additional instructions in **Chapter 21 -** "Useful Information"

Book Overview

1. I am going to walk you through the best way to understand how to create a residential cleaning company with efficiency and speed.

2. You will learn how important it is to choose the right entity and business model for your business. You will learn the need to protect yourself and create your own financial independence.

3. You will also learn from several big mistakes that people make when getting into a business and how you can avoid them to get ahead.

4. You will learn about my costly trial and error process and take important points from my 37 years of experience. I will help you identify the steps to create your niche market.

5. You will learn the importance of creating innovate selling points and differentiating yourself from the competition.

6. You will also learn how to focus on branding for your business.

7. You will learn the deal-breaking difference between you and your competition and understand that what you have to offer so you are always be in the mind of your target market.

8. You will receive a sample of a *Simple Proposal* for your cleaning services, including a very important, specific mention of non-compete agreement that you can sign with your client. This alone is worth owning this book.

9. You will receive a sample of non-compete agreement that is great to sign with your employee or subcontractor and is *a* must have if you hire any workers.

10. You will find many pricing solutions that are relevant to residential cleaning services.

11. In this book I will show you, how to be in business forever. Once they have dealt with your business, your clients will never want to go anywhere else.

Contents

Foreword

I would like to take you by the hand and lead you through the steps required to build a business. I will guide you from the inception of your idea of creating a business through to constructing a solid business structure that will provide you with a sustainable, profitable business. With this book you can grow a business, which you can work in, run, manage and create an Empire out of and if you wish, at some point, sell it for a healthy profit.

My book is for the beginners in residential cleaning services. In it you will find many similarities to commercial cleaning services, but my intention was not to mix information regarding commercial cleaning service and residential cleaning service procedures together and therefore not to complicate and overwhelm the process for those who are just starting in cleaning industry. My intention is to show you the steps to take how you can gain a complete understanding of this business and create your own financial freedom.

Let me take you back 37 years; I was new to the U.S.A., poor and hardly knew any English. I had an education in a totally unrelated field to the cleaning industry. At this point in time my education did not matter to me. What really mattered was that I could make enough money to pay my bills, put food on the table and create my own financial freedom.

I was looking for a business that would be safe from a recession, easily duplicated, repeatable (*so that for one successful transaction, you can have many repeated results with the one client),* and a business that was not depending only on my physical skills.

With this concept I started *Residential Cleaning Services*. I knew that if I needed more money, all I had to do is to get more clients. At first, I did this in my own available time and later, I progressed I hired another person to work for me.

The world has changed dramatically since I started my first cleaning service in 1981.

Life is more complicated now, more stressful and demanding - and so the need to become financially independent has become even more desirable.

I believe that in the near future robots and automation will replace many workers across many different industries, but I whole-heartedly believe that cleaning services will remain a business with a necessity for human touch and will remain free of major automation.

Because of the uncertainty in our world, so many people today are gripped with sense of fear and have insecurities about their future. They are afraid of losing their jobs. A logical response to this problem is to create your own business and with it you can create your own independence. In this book I offer some suggestions on developing the required skills that are easily obtained with your present abilities.

How you will apply this knowledge will vary greatly and will be determined by your unique strengths, talents and creativity. Ultimately, success in any endeavor derives from taking action combined with your determination from which you develop a burning desire to succeed.

With the rate of change in technology, there is an unprecedented increase in competition driven by globalization markets nationwide. Make no mistake - franchise companies are doing business in your neighborhood. As a result, we must not only be educated, we must re-educate ourselves on an ongoing basis. To avoid becoming obsolete, we must invest in and develop our core competencies. It is best to be backed by experience, not necessarily your own.

'Smart is that person who learn on their mistakes, but very smart is the one who learns off the mistakes of others'

- John Assaraf

Just remember that creating your own cleaning service is only your vehicle to financial freedom. It is important you use your business as a vehicle to develop your hobbies and have time for your family and the social life that you deserve.

We all strive to do our absolute best in our lives and our businesses. We try to hire the best people, create the best product or service and make the right decisions.

This book will help you to make the right decisions and minimize the risk in your life.

My intention is to lead you through an easy to apply process that will deliver you fast results.

For those of you who already have experience in cleaning other peoples' homes this book will show you how to start thinking like a business owner and an entrepreneur. We will guide you to take your first steps to creating a real business.

For those of you who never cleaned before, this book will give you a very good idea of whether this form of business is for you. You will learn a strong foundation to start any business, you will start thinking like a marketer and most importantly you will understand how to become successful in anything that you put your mind to.

No matter where you are coming from; your background, education, nationality or race, if you need to become financially free, this book will give you the ideas and direction of where to start your journey.

You may think, *'but this business is not for me, I am a collage graduate how can I stoop so low to become a cleaner?'*

The good news is that you don't have to become a cleaner or a janitor. Instead, decide to become a business owner, a leader, a manager and a force for good.

I know a few owners of janitorial companies that are lawyers and others who have graduated from financial colleges. As for me, I started my first residential cleaning company in the second year of emigrating to the U.S.A. from Poland. At that time, I did not even speak proper English. I had to prepare myself for each conversation based on my anticipated understanding what my prospective client may ask or say.

I prepared every possible question and every possible answer that would apply to what I was doing. We had no computers or Internet to help me in my communication skills. I had to use the telephone, pager or engage in a good old fashion face-to-face conversation.

Since then, I have sold my residential cleaning company and created commercial cleaning services, which I retained for several years. Eventually, I sold that for a profit and started another business *Clean Impressions Corp.* in the state of Illinois. This time I decided to keep my business for as long as I am living, and it remains profitable. I am well down the path in this journey and this year we are celebrating 20 years in business with this very company.

My story was published in a book, '*Business Inspirations of Polish Woman of the World*' with multiple authors. In this book there were 20 women from different parts of the world and in different fields of business. We all shared success in common We also wanted to help and inspire others to create their destiny, no matter what their circumstances are and no matter what barriers and difficulties they face.

This storytelling brought us together. We wanted to share our stories in the form of business inspiration. Our stories were written using our very real experiences and were based on our dreams, challenges, failures and struggles, as we were able to overcome the odds and turn our efforts into rich reward.

I know that there are other books available on how to create residential cleaning services so why should you like to reach out for my advice? **I know this industry and I know how to show you the easy steps to create your own residential cleaning service, backed by 36 years of experience**.

In my life, small business owners and those that desired to build their own businesses - from the ground up, have approached me regularly. I have been asked to become their mentor, to lead them through the startup process. In fact, I was asked so many times that I cannot possibly afford this much time to help them all.

I have helped several people through the years and for couple of years now I have kept saying that I will write a book using my knowledge, based entirely on my considerable experiences. Finally, now is the time has come and I can share with you my knowledge and experiences on how to start and run a successful residential cleaning company through the lessons I will teach you in this book.

Use it!

It is especially for you!

Chapter One

AVOID THESE MISTAKES

Learn the 5 biggest mistakes that people make that slow or paralyze their actions on the road to success.

I fully believe that if you can drop these 5 mistakes from your life, you will be on your way to success:

1) A lack of self-esteem and confidence

I am talking about the self-esteem issues that many people face that are already working in this profession. Quite simply, they don't believe that they can start a business.

The mindset of a lot of people in this industry is that they think that they don't know enough, or don't have enough resources, or that they don't have the credentials to create a business. This is such a wrong and disempowering belief. No one was born with all the skills and knowledge to run a business – these are all learnable skills.

When I started 37 years ago I did not have what it takes – I had very minimal language skills, no savings of any kind, no idea how to run a business and no special credentials. It would have been very easy for me to give up and believe that I wasn't good enough.

At this point in time, many people would have given me no chance to grow financially. I had no option to return to my native country of Poland.

Perhaps this saying is true, *'when it hurts enough you will find a way'.*

2) Procrastination

Procrastinating is the action of delaying or postponing something. It is never helpful in business.

3) Surrounding yourself with people that will drag you down

And they will! Every time that you talk to them about your business idea, or something that will progress you forward, they will throw their negative opinions at you. I learned early on in my business career, that when you play with people who are in a worse position then you are, you are never going to improve yourself.

A friend can kill your ideas. You don't need a lot of poison to kill someone, only a little bit. Just a little bit of poison from the wrong person at the wrong time can destroy months of work. In the end, you can get so disappointed and feel let down so many times that you have a hard time being able to get excited about anything anymore.

And the worst thing that can happen is that you don't believe in you anymore. People close to you will tell you *be realistic.* This is nothing but a fancy word for describing negativity.

People always will find something to criticize. Shut them out of your mind and if you need to, out of your life. Ask yourself, what do I want to become? Find those achieving what you want at a high level. Surround yourself with those who you want to become.

Find a mentor, someone that already did what you want to accomplish and ask questions. There is nothing more effective than learning from the experiences of someone that you would like to emulate. Spend time with them and get them in your life!

Who you spend time with, that is who you become.

4) Doing business with the sole focus on Money

We all want to have financial results. We are all looking for a good, solid and sustainable source of income – and cleaning services are a fantastic source of income.

I would like to point this out now, before you start your business, that money is only a symbol. You need to focus on your value and solving problems of others. The side effect of all that hard work is the money.

If you focus on the money, you will miss the boat. Ultimately, business is about what you can contribute to other peoples' lives.

5) Thinking negatively

Negative thinking is the worst thing that can happen to you in business. In my experience it is a power to destroy. But what being negative really means is that you are fearful. See life as it is - at face value and never worse that it is. Don't think of things that have been and gone. Focus on the things that are right in your life.

Can you live your life for 7 days without thinking negatively? When you face challenges, look at them in a way that you focus on the solution and not the problem.

I call this the 7-day mental challenge! See how you get on.

It is important to spend most of your time being positive or if that isn't possible, being negative in a positive way. Yet, just being positive is not enough. To be a success in business you also require action. You must be doing something to get you there, to make your dream happen. Armed with the information in this book by making even the smallest steps forward, you will get to your destination.

I am a big believer that the solution to a very uncertain future in the job market, is to own your own business. Think of it this way, you can't be fired or laid off because you own the business. An Oxford University study shows that 47% jobs in US are at risk of being replaced automated or eliminated in the next 20 years. Other studies say that computers will replace 80% of jobs within in two decades.

Thankfully, you need not to worry about this in the cleaning industry and you can start making money in residential cleaning. With the end goal in mind you will be able to afford new business ventures and pursue any hobbies that you desire.

As Napoleon Hill said,

'I am not perfect, but I am good. When I screw-up I make it better'

Chapter 2

ABOUT THE RESIDENTIAL CLEANING INDUSTRY

Learn the different forms of services that you can provide for your clients. After reading this chapter you will be able to decide which model of residential cleaning service is right for you.

Starting solo

One of the options of becoming a residential cleaner is to start solo. At this point in time you are becoming the cleaner and providing all the cleaning services yourself.

If somebody told you that this is an easy business to build, don't believe it.

This is as easy as starting any other business. It depends entirely on your skill set that you possess and the amount of knowledge that you already have and the amount of knowledge that you will learn - to make sure that those steps do become easy.

This business is physically demanding, especially if you start as a solo worker. However, starting in this fashion does have its benefits:

- Low cost at start-up, which can be a big help in starting a successful business.

- Your profit margins will be quite high, and you will generate cash flow daily. The biggest expense in this business is the cost of labor. It is important that as you begin to grow, that you keep a portion of your profits for future expansion.

- You can build the reputation of your company by your example.

- Doing the cleaning yourself will give you a very good idea how much time it takes to complete specific jobs.

- You will learn from experience how to price new jobs in the future and what to look for when you are visiting your customers' homes. You will become an expert in determining their cleaning needs.

Obtaining a business license as a solo worker

Business licenses are issued when you register your business entity with your state or county. A solo housecleaning business can register with the county clerk as a sole proprietor, known as *"doing business as" - (DBA).* For example, I could be DBA as *Your Name* Cleaning Services.

The DBA gives you the authority to advertise and operate as the business name but follows your personal tax identification number for all tax purposes.

In some instances, you need to apply for a business license and renew your business license each year in the city hall of the town that you conduct your business in (depending on the state and county*).* This applies no matter what business structure you are operating under.

Get licensed

It is important that you review the legal and administration requirements for your city, county and state to see what licenses

---

you may need to start a cleaning company. Everywhere is different. Some places do require a cleaning business to obtain an occupational license to register the business, whilst others simply require you to file a DBA form if you are operating the business under a name other than your own name.

While administration and setting up your business can be tedious, it is beneficial to think about the end goal. Picture the freedom from your 9-5 job, the very attractive hourly wage of $20-$45 per hour and being paid each working day that you perform your service.

As a side note, if you are operating out of Texas - if you form a company that does housekeeping services, you may need to charge a **sales tax** in some cases.

However, if you are considered self-employed and your work is limited to normal housekeeping without doing extra work like repairs, you may not need to charge sales tax.

Group cleaning services

This is where cleaning staff operates together as a crew. Each member of the crew specializes in one aspect of the cleaning process. This form of employment ensures that your employees work quickly with the highest degree of experience and quality.

The result of an organized group cleaning service is a team of professional cleaners, trained, uniformed, fully insured and bonded. It is important to create a team that knows the boundaries. A team that is trained well will not eat, drink, smoke, or operate any appliances while inside a client's property.

In this setup, you provide all the cleaning equipment and products. Except on the occasions where your client may have a specific product that they would like to use of their own. In this situation, you need to be informed in advance about the specific supply and method of using their product and give specific instructions to the manager of the crew. Clear communication should ensure that the manager of the crew recognizes the instances that they need to call the office manager. This will all depend on familiarity of the product and the procedures in place on how to use the product.

Cleaning supplies

You will also need several cleaning supplies. The most common cleaning supplies include:

- Glass cleaner

- Natural cleaners

- Bowl cleaner

- Vinegar

- Degreaser

- Gloves

- Trash bags

- Garbage can liners

- Spray bottles

- Buckets

- Mops

- Feather dusters

- Toilet brushes

- Paper towels

- Rags

- Squeegees

It might take time to decide the exact quantity of cleaning supplies that you need. As you gain more experience, you will have a better idea of how much to keep on hand.

Equipment

Some larger equipment is needed to start your business:

- An upright vacuum cleaner

- A backpack for details; or

- A detail hand vacuum cleaner, as residences will often require detail cleaning on request.

Individual household cleaning services

Individual household cleaning services occur when you schedule one person to clean each residence, with a minimum of 6 hours of service. In this instance, the client provides the supplies and equipment. These are the clients that prefer not to use anybody else's vacuum cleaners. They don't want to be exposed to other people's dust, germs and bacteria. They choose what cleaning solutions they want to be used in their homes and gladly rely on professionals, such as you, to give them recommendations on what to buy. It is the type of arrangement that when they are low on supplies, you would leave a note for them to purchase them in advance.

In this sort of cleaning arrangement, the cleaning services will be slightly lower in price, to reflect using the client's solutions and equipment.

This was my model of business when I first started my residential cleaning company. By the time that I sold my company I had 45 girls working for me. It is important to note that not every client likes to have a crew of people coming to clean their house.

To accommodate this situation and the needs of my clients, I developed a service named *Individual Cleaning System*. I had a van picking up my employees from one or two meeting spots in the city of Chicago and delivering them to my client's residences outside of the city in approximately the same geographical area. They all worked for 6 hours in each house. After the 6 hours of work, we picked our employees up and brought them back to the meeting place where they were picked up in the morning.

We had set price and a set amount of time for all the houses that we cleaned in our daily routes. If the house was larger and needed to be clean 2 times per week, the work schedule was adjusted accordingly.

Here is a working example for you:

Take a 5,000 + square foot house. It was cleaned on Mondays and Fridays. If there were no other instructions from the client on the day of services, then we followed the schedule that was set in initial agreement and in accordance to the client's specifications and needs. (Note: In this industry the client's requests should always supersede the regular schedule)

After 5 years in business I had three 15-passenger vans delivering employees to different areas of Chicago.

Non-Compete Agreements

At this point in time it is vital to raise a very important point. In order to save some frustrations in the future, I recommend that you sign a non-compete agreement with your client. This is to protect you from losing a client to your employee. **It is vital to keep it very short and simple. I provide a working example in the chapter 'Helpful Forms'.**

This is to protect you from losing your client to your employee.

Another important agreement to protect your clients is a Non-Disclosure Agreement – (NDA) signed by your employee, regarding your specific client's name and location. I am sure that your clients will appreciate this form of optional protection.

Combining both models - Individual and crew cleaning services

This is very good model because you can accommodate all the needs of your clients. When you grow your business to the point that you can afford to invest in purchasing one or more mini-vans, you can set it up in such way that one mini-van is servicing clients that prefer crew cleaning, while the other can manage individual service requests.

Once you have a crew setup then you can also accommodate 'on request' cleaning jobs, which included:

- Move-in / move-out cleaning,

- One-time cleaning of apartments or homes,

- Once a month repeated service; or

- After construction cleaning.

In my experience, many times we had to refuse cleaning services for not having the specific ability to assemble a crew, since all our employees worked on a regular, schedule basis.

If our clients were leaving for vacation or cancelled some days before their scheduled appointment for any reason - we had agreement that they will provide a replacement house (friends or family members home to be cleaned) or pay 50% of the fee if they wanted to ensure that the same person will come back to clean their home after they return. Of course, they didn't have to do that if they did not care about the change in person cleaning their home.

Franchise cleaning services

At this stage, is important to add in some additional facts to help improve awareness about franchises. Franchises require an initial investment but have the advantage of a recognized name, a workable formula for offering services and marketing techniques that are proven to work.

By starting out on your own, you save a lot of money in terms of initial expenses, but you must work out all the details for yourself - how to market your business, what to charge and how to get that really tough stain out of the carpet you are trying to clean.

To purchase a Franchise company for your location, you could be paying anywhere from $35,000 to about $150,000 and continue to pay 7%-10% monthly from your gross sales to the franchisor. The fees that you pay are for ongoing support and the marketing for the (usually nationwide) company.

They will teach you how to clean. For most franchises you need to follow a cleaning system that is the same across the entire company, in the form of tutorials and hands-on instructions.

Franchises expect you to follow their guidance right down to the tiniest detail. While this ensures a consistent image and service for the franchise, it eliminates any chance for your creativity and putting forward your own ideas for growth. There are restrictions and requirements on what kind of vehicle you must own to operate business and you get directives on how to equip your vehicle to be ready to perform services.

Some franchise companies have restrictions regarding your office location for your business, including how to set-up your office. Franchise ownership does not necessarily guarantee large profits. If another franchise within your parent company experiences customer problems, negative reviews or legal issues, this may affect your business as well, due to the name association.

If this form of business model is for you, please research extensively and do your due diligence. Then consider the pros and cons of owning a franchise-based business before deciding.

Now that you know which model of the services you will provide, you are ready to take the next step forward.

Case Study

While writing this book I was asked a question: 'How can I replace myself from working alone and take it to the next level - a managerial position, if I have only one account per day?'

This question came from a single mother that started a business and could not afford to add another client to her daily schedule because she needed to pick up her daughter from kindergarten every day.

This is how I see this situation:

Let's say for example, you have 6 days a week cleaning arrangement. A good starting point would be to talk to two clients out of that six and say that you need time out for a while and you will search for the right person to replace you. Inform both clients that you will train your replacement and that you will check if they are happy with her and that you will check regularly on this girl's performance.

If for some reason they don't like her or how she cleans for them, you will make sure you will find someone else. At the same time, you will explain to them that you value them as your client and you want to retain them.

Explain to your clients that you will bring them an agreement indicating how often this service will be performed, including some cancellation rules, the price of service and a copy of your insurance so they feel secure that they will be covered just in case anything happens.

Usually the girls don't carry any insurance, it will be up to you should you decide to give them this protection, typically it will be because you like to create long-term relationship. Generally, the insurance that you provide is liability insurance, workmen compensation and bonding.

Secondly, find a qualified person to hire, bring her with you to the two different clients homes. Train her to meet your client's needs and expectations. Once they approve that they like the girl that you hired, ask them to give you referrals so the girl that is now working for them will become busy every day and have enough work to fill an entire week. This will also ensure that she will gladly stay working for you.

Before you introduce your new hire to the client, you need to sign with your employee a contract or subcontract agreement (if the law in your state permits), that states what account you are providing and name and address of the client. In the subcontract agreement make sure to include a provision about the non-compete status with your company. ***You will find a sample of the non-compete agreement in the Useful Forms chapter.***

Now, when you replace yourself for those two days you can concentrate on getting new clients (for your new hire first) so she has more reason to stay and work for you.

Repeat this process.

It is important that you reschedule those 2 working days to be free of work. At this point in time, provide new clients with an agreement including your non-compete and proof of insurance. Ensure your new hire also signs her agreements.

You should now be free to go to the new client's home and train the girl there. Show her how to satisfy her obligations and responsibilities in the agreement with your client. This will insure that your new client will be happy with the performance.

A few things will happen as a result: One - is that you are making sure that the client will get everything that you promised. Two - is that you will get to know the new account very well. Three - is that you are building a bond with a new client, and like your new hire, you will know exactly what to do on this account.

All agreements should be very simple and quite short in their provisions. The most important parts of the agreement are that both parties know what is expected of them, how much it will cost, the remedies if one side is not very happy and proof of insurance for both parties' protection.

Chapter 3

BUSINESS STRUCTURE: YOUR TYPE OF ENTITY

*In this Chapter you will learn about the **three steps** to get you started with your residential cleaning services. After reading this chapter you will be ready to choose your business structure, your business name and be able to make it all legal.*

Step One - Choose the business structure.

- How to differentiate structures of your business, so that one of them will become the most suited for you. This includes the need for personal protection from possible future misfortunes and business liabilities.

Step Two - Choose your business name.

- What are the most important things that you must consider, when choosing the name of your future business.

Step Three - Make it legal.

- How simple it can be to make your business legal? It is a very easy process that you can do yourself or by hiring a law firm.

We have already covered the type or business model that will suit your business. You already know which model of business is appealing to you and you have thought about the future scaling of your business. You should already know whether you will you work solo, build a company to grow, keep it for future generations, or sell it for a profit? There is nothing hard about this process.

"Nothing is particularly hard if you divide it into small jobs"

- Henry Ford

Step One - Choose the Business Structure.

It is important that you take time to learn, understand and choose the entity of your future business before you file for your business license.

When you are starting a business without any employees, you can operate a very simple structure as a sole proprietor. However, when you intend to hire other people to work for you, then you need to consider a different business structure like S-corporations or LLC.

Here's a quick look at the differences between the most common forms of business entities: sole proprietor, partnership corporation and limited liability company (LLC). The type of business entity you decide on will depend on three primary factors: liability, taxation and record keeping.

1) A sole proprietor - This is the most common form of business. It's easy to form and offers complete managerial control to the owner. However, the owner is also personally liable for all financial obligations of the business.

When you choose to start as a sole proprietor as your legal structure and the name of your company, (E.g. *Your Name* Cleaning Services) you will not be doing business as someone else and no additional registration is necessary.

When you choose other name for your business than your own, (E.g. ABC Cleaning Services), you will be doing business as (DBA) under an assumed name and you need to file a fictitious name statement in your county.

Depending on the state and which county you are registering your business, the requirements may vary. Usually the law requires that a sole proprietor register other than the real name of the persona, in the county clerk's office. The purpose of the law is to place on public record the name of the person who is conducting or transacting a business under an assumed name. There is a small fee to file and this includes the cost of advertising in a local newspaper for a few weeks. You will get specific instructions on how to word this message to the public, informing them that you will be doing business under an assumed name.

There is no fee to start as a sole proprietor and no renewal fee each year – that applies to other forms of entities.

2) A corporation – A corporation becomes an entity, separate from those who have founded it. A person handles the responsibilities of the organization. Like a person, the corporation can be taxed and can be held legally liable for its actions. The corporation can also make a profit. **The key benefit of corporate status is to avoid personal liability.** The primary disadvantage is the cost to form a corporation, yearly renewal charge, and the extensive record keeping that is required.

The S Corporation - The S Corporation is more attractive to small-business owners than a standard corporation. That is because an S Corporation has some appealing tax benefits and still provides business owners with the liability protection of a corporation. With an S Corporation, income and losses are passed on to shareholder(s) and included on their individual tax returns. As a result, there is just one level of federal tax to pay.

3) A partnership- This organizational structure involves two or more people who agree to share in the profits or losses of a business. A primary advantage is that the partnership does not bear the tax burden of profits or the benefit of losses. Instead, profits or losses are 'passed through' to partners to report on their individual income tax returns. A primary disadvantage of this structure is the liability - each partner is personally liable for the financial obligations of the business.

4) **Limited Liability Company -** A hybrid form of partnership, the limited liability company (LLC), is gaining in popularity because it allows owners to take advantage of both the partnership and the corporation. The advantage of this business format is that profits and losses can be passed through to the owners without the need to tax the business itself, while the owners are shielded from personal liability.

Ultimately, the decision you make on your type of legal structure, is one that you don't want to make alone. Get advice from a specialist about the ideal organizational structure to take. Small Business Administration in your state will have all this information available for you. Then you can talk to your CPA or accountant. It can make a huge difference later. In business, as in life, one size rarely fits all. This decision has an impact on how much you pay in taxes and it will affect the amount of paperwork your business is required to do and the personal liability you face.

Choosing to start an S-Corporation, sole ownership, or C-Corporation will separate your business from your personal assets and reduces your personal liability. If someone sues your company, your business assets and personal assets are not considered interchangeable.

You can register for a limited liability company or corporation through the secretary of state. Fees vary but are more expensive for LLC or corporate registration versus a DBA.

Step Two - Choose your business name.

The most important things to remember when choosing a name is how memorable the name is, your target market, and your plans for the future vision of the company. Then you need to take the personal approach, *"Your Name Cleaning Service"*, or the more impersonal, *"ABC Cleaning Services"*.

Before settling on your chosen name, check that you can get a matching domain for your website and e-mail address. It will appear odd if your company name, the address of your website and your email are completely different.

If you find that someone else is using the same name, it is time to do some research. Find out how long they have been using that name. If they have been in business for a long time, you might want to change your assumed name so there is no confusion for the public. Filing your business name does not create substantive rights to the use of that name.

Regardless of which business registration you choose, you will need to search the secretary of state's database to confirm your business name doesn't conflict with other businesses.

Remember that the name you choose will become a key element of your overall marketing plan. Use some creativity when coming up with your business name. While choosing a name, do not forget that at some point in your business ownership, you may decide that you would like to sell your business. If you name your business with your initials, first, or last name, then someone who will purchase your business will keep that name. It will not add to the value of your business if you have a personal name.

Start brainstorming ideas based on common perceptions or requirements that clients have when it comes to hiring a cleaning company. The main task is to focus on the business of securing clients. It is important to make sure your potential and existing clients can recall your cleaning business name quickly. A catchy name that rhymes is one option to consider.

Using a short descriptive phrase of about two or three words is also helpful. Try to include the word *clean, cleaning services, service* or a synonym in the company name. For example, "*For the Love of Cleaning*" and "*Royal Cleaning Services*" are catchy names that describe a cleaning business and are easy to recall.

Another idea is to narrow down your specific focus of the cleaning business by adding residential to the name. For instance, "*Izia`s Residential Cleaning Company*" indicates that this is a company that specializes in residences and apartments.

When a potential customer searches through the Internet for house cleaning services, seeing the word residential in your name may set your cleaning company apart from the others.

According to the *House Cleaning Tips* website, using your own name, such as "*Teresa's Cleaning Service*", is not usually a good idea, as it will not make much of an impression on potential customers. Once again **don't forget to check to make sure the name you choose hasn't already been taken**.

Step Three - Make it legal

When you finally choose your business entity and the name, now is the time to make sure you are operating legally.

Licensing for House cleaning:

Being licensed refers to registering the business entity with the state, which allows you to legally do business in the state.

Do you need a business license?

There is no specific license required to be a house cleaner. For most house cleaning services, you won't need any other special licensing or permits to conduct day-to-day operations. This form of business does not utilize harsh cleaning agents that are regulated by the Environmental Protection Agency. However, if you are unsure about the products and quantities you use, contact your local EPA office or city council about your permit requirements.

Before you create your business as a legal entity, it is important to note that you don't need any certifications to open a residential or commercial cleaning company.

In the future as you become an expert in an area such as I did with my business, you may want to obtain specific certifications to become an authority in any specific fields. This will be when you decide that specializing in something is going to give you a competitive advantage.

To learn more - go to your local IRS/ business site to gain more information about this and helpful business topics, including filing for employer ID numbers.

Each State will have an option of checking if your assumed name is available. **Do this before you start your business registration**. To check if the business name is taken or not, go to the secretary of state website and insert your business name to check for its availability.

If you decide to be incorporated, file an assumed name with the state that your business is residing in—the same applies to your Articles of Incorporation.

If you need the name to be filed quickly, you may file using the electronic filing system in your State. There you will find the instructions and application for filing electronically. When you apply online you will get your EIN number immediately. If you prefer to complete form SS-4 and fax it to the service center of your state, then they will usually respond with a return fax in about one week.

There is a fee to incorporate and set up a LLC Company and with that comes a renewal fee for each successive year. The fees vary depending on the state that you are in.

Once you obtain your EIN number you can set-up a business checking account at your local bank. It is important to note that the bank should not be advising corporations to file at the county. From my experience the bank has ability to check and verify this information right away.

Chapter 4

DO YOU NEED A LAW FIRM?

This Chapter is to show you that it is OK to learn how to apply and fill in all the forms on your own. I did! You will learn about the costs associated with forming the legal status of your company and about bi-laws and whether you need them.

I am not an attorney and will not even begin to give you legal advice. I will advise you that you can learn anything. However, if you are not sure about the legal process or uncomfortable with filing for a new company EIN number, by all means, do use professional to help you with this. Consult with your lawyer or accountant. Just to give you an idea, it will cost you approximately $50-$800 including the state fee. It all depends on the state that you are in and law firm that you use.

With the technology we have available now, basic legal advice is available online. Now you can get legal forms where you can choose the document you need and just fill in the blanks. The result is that you will have your own customized legal document. Today, technology has helped our life became so much easier without spending a lot of money for it.

I remember spending $1800 just for sub-contract agreement with a sales director that I hired about 10 years ago and spending $400 for a letter of intent to purchase a business. Now you will spend $20-$50 depending on the company that you use online. With the globalization of services, law firms are creating online services that will eliminate the necessity to interact with their offices and ask for their services. The good thing for business owners is that it saves you time and money.

So, if you study law, stop immediately. There is going to be 90% less lawyers in the future, only specialists will remain.

You can use Legalzoom.com, Rocket Lawyer Incorporated, or Inc.File.com to create any document including corporate by-laws, articles of corporation for your S-Corp or C-Corp. If you created an LLC, then you can learn more about your needs of creating an operating agreement.

Costs related to your new business

Some costs of creating and running a business are essential, and should be expected, while other costs are optional. Optional costs can be delayed until you are running income-producing activities and your cash flow can sustain in the costs. For example, there is no need to buy a bookkeeping program from the outset. Do your bookkeeping in a journal, either electronically, or keep it traditional with a simple pencil, paper and adding machine.

Expect onetime expenses:

It is important to cater for one off expenses such as legal and professional fees that relate to set-up. Purchases such as a vehicle, uniforms, accounting program, computer, telephone and office set-up costs, including office supplies.

On-going expenses:

These are recurring expenses such as your salary, your workers (when you have them), business insurance, car insurance, Internet, telephone charges, rent, utilities and cleaning solutions - if you are providing them in your business model.

By-laws

What are corporate by-laws, and do you need them?

Corporate by-laws are the internal rules of your company. They create the structure and rules that will guide how your business operates and apply to everyone involved including shareholders, executives and your employees. They are in place so that everyone will be on the same page. Depending on your type of business, you may or may not need to establish corporate by-laws, but most states require them for corporations (both S-Corps and C-Corps).

There are five states that require LLC's to create an operating agreement. These are Delaware, California, New York, Missouri, and Maine. If you're an LLC in other state, creating an operating agreement may not be required, but it will help to protect your business.

If you do not create your own operating agreement, your state already has a set of default rules that regulates all businesses, and this will apply to your business. By choosing and creating your own by-laws, you can override these state rules providing that your own rules are not against the law. It is much better to create your customized internal rules and processes specific to the unique needs of your company.

Chapter 5

YOUR BUSINESS PLAN

Here you will get few ideas how to create your business plan.

Do you need a Business Plan?

The short answer: Yes, you do!

Without a design plan, you would not build a home. Just like without a map or navigation system, you will not get to your desired destination. You don't want to do things on a 'whatever happens' basis. You need specific outcomes for the effort that you put in. Let's plan for it!

Don't be afraid of this process. This is simply a plan to do business. You need a plan to turn your business idea into a reality. Just like a builder needs a blueprint to build a house, this same idea applies to you.

A business plan is a blueprint that will guide your business from the start-up phase through its establishment and eventually into a phase of business growth. It doesn't have to be complicated in the beginning.

Let's make it simple! What if you would NOW equip yourself with a paperboard and make this **first business plan** as a visualization board?

> *"A DREAM written down with a date becomes a GOAL.*
>
> *A Goal broken down into Steps becomes a PLAN.*

A Plan backed by ACTION becomes REALITY"

On this visualization board you can start with the name of your business right in the middle of it. Don't have a name yet? No problem call it, *"My Residential Cleaning Services"* and you can change this later.

To proceed with your first business plan, you may want to ask yourself these questions followed by research on these topics:

- What is the reason that you are starting this company?

- Is there a need for your anticipated services?

- Who needs it?

- What is your target market?

- Are there other companies offering similar services?

- What is the competition like?

- How does your business fit into the market?

- Can you become unique in your market by offering a better service and creating more value for your clients?

"Business is nothing else, but Innovation and Marketing"

- Tony Robbins

Use this Idealizing Strategy.

Imagine that you have a magic wand. Imagine that you have all the resources, all the ability, all the skills and all the money to be able to market to your ideal client. What would your strategy look like? If your business were perfect in 3-5 years what would it look like? Create a vision about your business - what would you like the newspaper to say about you in 3-5 years` time?

If you could dictate the story what would you say? What are the words that your clients would use when they describe you? Do they say that you are the best?

Once you have those answers, you can focus on the WHY. Draw on your board another square or circle with the reasons WHY are you planning your business.

As my first mentor *John Assaraf* use to say, '*WHY, is more important then WHAT.*'

If you have a strong enough WHY, you will accomplish your goal. Add your burning desire (according to *Napoleon Hill*) and combine it with your definiteness of purpose – and by making even the smallest steps every day you will get closer to your goal and your success will be evident. With this formula, you can accomplish anything that you desire.

It is time to start planning your vision board.

To get to this point is already very rewarding. You will be overcome with a feeling of accomplishment and pride - now you are on your way to become a business owner.

And you should be very proud of yourself – **celebrate** this fact!

Chapter 6

BUSINESS INSURANCE

This chapter will show you 3 different forms of insurance that are very important and serve to protect you and your business.

It is not mandatory for cleaning businesses to be bonded and insured but it is a very important preventive activity to protect your business from damage, harm, theft or other issues with employees or the locations you work.

Business insurance helps you minimize the financial impact of common exposures. Without insurance, one major loss could put you out of business. Remember, your clients' homes are their most valued possession, with all their precious belongings in it.

You want to make them feel comfortable about your business and be someone who provides peace of mind and an assurance that they made a great decision by hiring you.

When you have insurance, potential customers gain more confidence by knowing that a cleaning company has taken extra steps to protect its customers and their belongings.

It is a good idea to obtain your business bond through a local insurance or surety Bond Company. Shop around to make sure that, with the same coverage, and different deductibles, that your premium will be affordable.

You can change the deductible amount later when you get more business. If you start hiring additional people, make sure that you purchase Worker's Compensation. This will protect you, by providing coverage for employees who are injured on the job. Laws in most states require workers' compensation coverage.

General liability - General liability insurance pays for your defense and any resulting damages if your service causes damage or harm. It can also cover medical bills – it is important to check the scope of your coverage. In a traditional insurance policy, where you pay a premium, if a loss occurs - the insurance company pays the loss as you move forward, and you don't need to repay the insurance company.

Commercial auto - Commercial auto insurance is important if you or your employees drive company cars or personal vehicles during the course of business. This coverage is essential because auto accident claims can be extremely expensive.

Make sure that your insurance amounts are at least at minimum required standards in your state.

Obtaining a Business Bond

Should you get bonding even if you are working yourself?

A surety bond is a specialty product offered by insurance companies and bond companies. Call your local insurance agent if you are unsure where to begin.

When trying to get new clients, it will be very helpful to show your client a proof of insurance and bonding. A bond is less expensive then liability insurance but the company issuing the bond expects to be repaid after a loss. The benefit of the bond is speed and assurance in paying the client.

Because the bond company expects repayment, the application process requires financial documentation. The application includes your business entity information, your contact details and a financial statement. After the insurance company reviews and approves your application, pay the bond fee. You will then receive a bond certificate.

When asked for proof of insurance, you don't present a copy of the insurance. Instead, ask your insurance company for a summary of your policy, which will serve as proof of insurance, indicating the specific insurance coverage that you have and the specific limits of your insurance.

Chapter 7

SETTING-UP YOUR OFFICE

In this chapter we discuss ideas on what are the most important items to obtain in your first few months of starting a business.

Congratulations! You have a business. You are probably asking, *'What do I do now?'*

What do you need to start your office?

The basics of your cleaning business at its bare minimum are a car and a smartphone with an Internet connection.

You should setup your office location somewhere that doesn't cost you a fortune. At the beginning a lot of small businesses opt to start their business from home. Until I purchased a building in a commercial location, all my businesses that I started were initially conducted from home.

For your office space you will need a desk, computer, Internet connection and a laser printer/copier/scanner. If you don't have a scanner in your printer there is no need to worry. You can download an app for your phone called CS - CamScanner. When you take a picture of a document or anything that you like to keep in your file it will save it to your file and you will have it accessible on the phone if you need it. It is also great to send documentation via email, or on other forms of social networking and you can do the same for business cards, receipts, invoice-bills, any pictures and hand-written notes or ideas, Soon, only few years from now, new smart phones will have 3D scanning possibilities.

Office supplies - things you need:

- Computer
- Cleaning supplies
- Cleaning equipment
- Marketing materials
- Website
- Email address
- Telephone – It helps not just to have a mobile but it helps your business to create a sense of credibility and stability by having a landline.
- Paper, stapler, clipboards,
- A desk calendar; and
- A book that you can make notes in.

While setting up your office, it is a good time to create a script on how to answer the phone. Practice what you will say during your initial meeting with client. Become a very good listener and make notes.

Is my car appropriate for my new business?

Any car will do if it's clean and if is not a luxury car. I had a situation once when I was growing my individual cleaning services - I was driving one of my employees to clean a client's house. My client was in front of the house when I arrived. Her reaction to my new Oldsmobile station wagon was, *"business must be good if you are driving a better car then mine."* She said this in such way that made me feel ashamed that I had bought the new car. I felt really bad. My enthusiasm for having a new car immediately shattered into pieces.

I answered with a very light and friendly tone of voice and with a gentle smile on my face. I said, *"This is exactly what you get when you are providing a dedicated and superior service. Besides, I spend 14 hours a day working, so I thought I will combine business and pleasure together and I got this car to see the results."*

My client was not working at the time and was a stay at home mom. Another client had recommended her, and I knew that this news would not go down so well and would spread really fast in the neighborhood we we're cleaning. I was becoming very nervous about the possible repercussions. Some of my clients simply congratulated me on my new car. However, after this experience I knew that I needed to stay in line and not make my clients think that maybe they are paying me too much.

My advice to you is this; stick with the average car, but make sure it's always clean. If your market niche is in the upper neighborhood, then you can justify having a nice, newer car - it is more important to always have it clean. Your car should reflect your clientele, so in this situation you would not want an old car that is scratched or has signs of fender-bender indents in it.

Chapter 8

ACCOUNTING

In this chapter we will discuss the importance of record keeping for all the activities in your business and you will learn some tax-deductible expenses that can make a difference in your record keeping for your next tax season.

My first and most important piece of advice on accounting is to outsource all accounting and payroll services. However, it is also important that you personally get a basic idea of tax obligations in your state, taking under consideration the entity that you have chosen to operate under.

Work alongside your accounting professional

I highly recommend that you learn how to keep good financial records in cooperation with your CPA or accountant. Keep track of your invoices and expenses and do not mix personal and business expenses – In my experience it is far simpler to keep them separate. Another important point is to be sure to save all your receipts for all that you spend on your business set-up and operations, as this is tax deductible.

As discussed earlier, there are apps like Shoe-boxed and CS - CamScanner, that allow you to take pictures of receipts and store them digitally.

If you would like to do your own bookkeeping and eventually hire someone to do it for you in your office, then I recommend the Quick Books program, which is used by all CPAs and

Accountants. When you need to deliver your bookkeeping for tax preparation, you just send to your accountant a copy of your Quick Books file.

Like every program, you need to get to know it a little. There are plenty of tutorials on how to set up and use this program. You no longer must go to school to learn how to use such a program and your accountant will answer all your questions that are specific to your company needs - such as what categories to use in your business to describe your expenses.

Here are your tax-deductible expenses: - Save any receipts for:

- Company setup fees, renewal fees, dues and subscriptions
- Uniform purchases and the cost of washing them
- Keep your miles logged in a mileage book every time you use your car for business
- Car purchases for business use – such as maintenance, repairs, plate stickers
- Car washes
- Parking
- Gasoline
- Office equipment
- Office supplies
- Cleaning supplies
- Cost of education related to business

Chapter 9

USEFUL FORMS

In this chapter we cover several helpful forms that will get you started and help you efficiently run a business. You will also find ideas on how to create your own employee handbook and find other useful resources that are great to have.

Disclamer :

Please check your local laws on providing non-compete agreement, non-disclosure agreement & subcontract agreement. The forms that I am providing are only suggestions, to help you determine which forms you may need and to simplify your road to create your successful business.

It is imperative that you have a **handbook** of company policies and procedures for your employees. Even if it is only a handful of pages long, you need to create questions and answers to many procedures and circumstances that may arise in certain work situations:

Here are examples of what you can include in your handbook:

- Where to report and arrive for work:

- At the office?

- Onsite?

>   - At a common location?

>   - At what time?

- What is the contact information needed for a job:

- The first person to call in event of any problem or questions.

- Then the next person to call and so on

- Dress code and what is acceptable to be worn:

- Uniforms?

- Smocks or aprons?

- What colors?

- White shirt and jeans?

- Include the quality and condition of clothes. No stains or tears.

- Cleanliness of uniforms and how will you reimburse staff for upkeep?

- Will you have dry cleaning delivery every week for the supply of uniforms?

- Will you add some amount to your staff wages as a clothing allowance?

- Lunch time break

– For how long and at what time?

- Client interaction Policy

– It can be a good idea to have this written down. Here is an example script:

'If there is a client at home while cleaning, staff should keep their conversation short and polite, with a smile on your face. It is nice to interact with pleasantries while remembering the task at hand. Avoid conversations that discuss sensitive topics such as politics,

religion, the client's personal lives and your own personal grievances.'

Residential Client Information Form

This information sheet can be used for gathering vital client information over the phone or in person.

Name_____

Address_____

Phone #_____

Another phone #_____

Home _____Apartment _____Condo

_____Other_____

Square footage_____

Number of Levels/ Floors_____

Number of bathrooms_____

Number of bedrooms_____

How many Rooms Total _____

Children _____Ages_____ How many_____

Pets _____Yes _____No_____ Type

_____

After Approval:

Home Security _____Yes _____No_____

Code_____

Emergency Number_____

Secondary # if not answered

_____

Home security additional instructions

_____

_____

_____

House Key _____Yes _____No_____ How many?

_____

Received (date) _____

Print Name

_____

Returned Clients House Key

(date)_____

Print Name _____

Residential Quote Form

This residential quote form is excellent for walkthroughs with a client. Use a clipboard to fill in this sheet with vital information about the client's home and needs.

Clients Name_____

Address_____

Phone_____

E-mail_____

Fax_____

Date_____

Sales Persons Name _____

House _____ Apartment _____Move-in _____Move-out _____

Other_____

_____

_____

Square Footage _____

Frequency of Cleaning Services: Weekly _____Biweekly

_____Monthly_____

Other _____

Desired Days and Time to schedule:

_____

Approved Days and Time

_____

Services Requested:

Initial cleaning _____Yes _____No

_____

Basic Routine Cleaning _____ Yes

_____No_____

Deep Cleaning

_____

Additional Cleaning _____Yes _____No _____

Details_____

_____

_____

_____

Special instructions from the Client:

Estimated hours_____ Rate per

Hour_____

Cleaning Supplies ___Yes

_____No_____

Equipment ___Yes _____No

_____

Payment Method

_____

Preparing a Proposal

Based on this information gathered during a home visit - using the *Residential Quote Form*, you will be able to prepare a proposal. It is important to specify services that you will provide, including your *non-compete* agreement.

- Make sure you include with your proposal:
- A list with a description of basic services that you will provide.
- Any other services that you agreed to provide in addition.
- Include vital information about your service - like what day of the week, how often and the time frame that the work will be completed.
- What supplies, and equipment are included?
- What supplies, and equipment are not included? If they are not included, then indicate those supplies and equipment that are provided by the client.
- Include in your proposal a Menu for additional cleaning services - at the request of the client only.
- A non-compete agreement.
- Sign and date your proposal.
- Indicate where your client should sign and date it.
- Make room to display your starting date of services.
- Include your proof of insurance.

_____

_____

Logo of your Co. or just Company Name
Address, phone number, e-mail, website

Date:

Client Name that You are addressing this Agreement

Proposal/Agreement for cleaning

Your Company Name will provide cleaning services in your residence per attached specifications and per following terms:

Service charge: Based on one (*1*) time per week cleaning on (*Fridays*), charge for each cleaning visit will be $_____

On major holidays such as New Year, Easter, Memorial Day, 4Th of July, Labor Day, Thanksgiving, and Christmas no services will be performed. However, if holiday falls on that day we will call in advance to schedule cleaning on alternative day.

Duration of Agreement and termination: This agreement shall be in effect as of the date of _____

And will continue on weekly basis but may be terminated by either party upon giving 7 days' written notice by e-mail to the other party.

Any adjustment to this agreement would have to be mutually agreed.**Billing schedule**: *Describe how you like to be paid and when*

When the additional service is rendered or when the supplies are sold (if applicable) we will issue an invoice that will be due and payable within (5) days of the invoice. Each invoice will be billed to your home location where the services are provided.

If different please specify_____

Your Co Name reserves the right to charge late fee of $__ on all late payments. *Your Co. Name* may terminate services at any time without notice, for non-payment. In the event, of default on payments, Client agrees to pay collection costs.

Proposal / Agreement Page 1 of 2

Supplies and Equipment: *Who provides supplies and equipment?*

Personnel

We will provide experienced backup or emergency personnel should normally schedule personnel be unable to work.

Client agrees that during the term of this agreement and for Two (2) Years thereafter will not employ, or permit to be employed, any person who has performed services under this agreement at client's home.

Client   Signed by: _____   Date   Signed: _____

Your Company   Signed by: _____ Date Signed: _____

Proposal / Agreement Page 2 of 2

Service refusal note for non-payment

Your Company Name

Address

E-mail

Phone number

Today's Date

Dear Client,

I have shown up for work today and see that you did not leave a check for your last cleaning that I performed on _____ day, I hope it's not because you are not happy with my performance. If you are, please let me know.

Just in case that you may be unhappy with my service, I do not want to continue and make you disappointed again. Therefore, I did not clean today. Please note that you are liable for the non-payment and non-cancellation of services charged to the amount of $50.

Please contact me at your earliest convenience to remedy this situation, or to cancel your services, as per our agreement, dated _____.

Sincerely,

Your name_____

A list of services when you order:

Routine basic cleaning

Bedroom, Living Room & Common Areas

- Dust all accessible furniture surfaces - some shelf units may not be able to be dusted, depending on its contents.

- Wash and polish woodwork and baseboards - time may not permit you to wash and polish woodwork and baseboards on your first visit, but they can be maintained thereafter, usually one room per visit.

- Wipe down all mirrors and glass fixtures.

- Dust stairs, banisters and railings.

- Clean or dust outside of fireplace and mantel.

- Vacuum and wash all floor surfaces in the entire home – except for garages. Make sure you do not move china cabinets or dressers.

- High dust the ceilings for cobwebs, generally up to 8 feet.

- Dust hanging light fixtures and fans.

- Spot clean walls, doorjambs and clean light switches for fingerprints.

- Take out garbage and recycling.

Bathroom Cleaning

- Wash and sanitize the toilet, shower, tub and sink.

- Dust all accessible surfaces.

- Wipe down all mirrors and glass fixtures. Spray with professional cleaner and wipe dry – make sure your client advises you if the mirrors should not be directly sprayed with cleaner. Mirrored walls require additional time. Don't clean ceiling mirrors.

- Clean all floor surfaces.

- Take out garbage and recycling.

Kitchen Cleaning

- Wipe down outside of oven, refrigerator, cabinets and countertops.

- Shine sink and appliances.

- Wipe down furniture.

- Clean all floor surfaces.

- Take out garbage and recycling.

Extras

For a deeper clean, consider adding one or more cleaning extras. Most cleaning extras add (depending on the size) a minimum of half an hour of time and cost to your booking.

- Inside cabinets

- Inside fridge.

- Inside freezer - must be defrosted.

- Inside oven.

- Dust window blinds.

- Clean hanging light fixtures and fans.

- Laundry wash and dry.

- Interior windows.

- Screen cleaning.

A list of services when you order:

Deep Cleaning Service

Every deep clean includes the **basic clean** in detail and focuses on larger build ups, including the following:

- Washing ceiling fan blades. *

- Light fixtures - hand washed in place/not removed. *

- Blinds and shutters - vacuumed or washed *, mini-blinds dusted and washed. *

- Moldings, woodwork, and windowsills - hand washed or wiped. *

- Baseboards - hand washed or wiped (those reachable without moving furniture).

- Lamps and lampshades - dusted or vacuumed with brush attachment.

- Pictures and knick-knacks - hand wiped.

- Furniture - polished, fronts, sides, legs and/or vacuumed.

- Stovetop and drip pans scrubbed.

- All cabinet fronts cleaned.

- All exterior and interior doors washed.

- Light switch plates washed.

- Countertops and backsplashes washed.

- Mirrors - cleaned all the way to the top – (don't clean ceiling mirrors). *

- Tub/Shower tiles - detail scrubbed if build up

- Wastebaskets - emptied/washed/relined.

- Beds - change sheets and remake.

- Stairs – if carpeted vacuum, if wood simply wash.

- Floors - vacuumed and/or mopped, including closets.

- Detail vacuum all carpet areas including under the beds.

*We have a regulation to not climb higher than a 2-step ladder, as it is not covered by our insurance. Higher items can be dusted with an extension duster.

A list of services when you order:

Move in/out Service

If you specialize in move-in/move-out cleans then here are some ideas:

We specialize in move in/out of home cleaning services and small office cleaning.

Detailed move in/out cleaning services include everything in a routine cleaning and much more. They are perfect for making your new home or office sparkling clean and sanitized. Choose our heavy duty, detailed top to bottom cleaning for your spring clean. Services can be done on your house, office, apartment or condo.

This checklist is useful for every move-in/ move-out job to check out the progress.

It is a good idea to provide your crew with a copy, to make sure that all duties are fulfilled:

House cleaning services checklist for a move in/out:

Living Areas & Bedrooms:

- General dusting.

- Carpets vacuumed and edged.

- Windowsills cleaned – excluding glass.

- Baseboards dusted and wiped down.

- Vacuum, mop and dry hard floor surfaces.

- Stairs vacuumed.

- Flat areas damp cloth dusted.

- Leaving rooms appearing spotless.
- Remove cobwebs.

Bathroom:

- Tile walls and bathtubs cleaned and disinfected.
- Shower and shower doors cleaned and disinfected.
- General dusting.
- Carpets vacuumed and edged.
- Windowsills cleaned.
- Baseboards dusted and wiped down.
- Mirrors cleaned and shined.
- Sink and counters cleaned and disinfected.
- Floors washed and disinfected.
- Clean and disinfect toilet.
- Clean and shine chrome fixtures.
- Wipe down inside/outside of cabinets and drawers.
- Cobwebs removed.

Kitchen:

- Sinks cleaned and disinfected.
- Countertops cleaned and disinfected.
- Clean inside/outside of cabinets and drawers.
- Clean exterior of large appliances.
- Baseboards dusted and wiped down.

- Clean small countertop appliances.

- Clean exterior of the refrigerator.

- Outside of range hood cleaned.

- Top and front of range cleaned.

- Drip pans cleaned.

- Chrome shined.

- Wipe down inside and outside of microwave.

- Thorough dusting throughout.

- Clean table and chairs.

- Floors vacuumed and mopped.

- Trash emptied.

- Cobwebs removed.

Noncompete Agreement

This agreement is between *(Your Co. Name)* _____,(Employer),

and Name _____ (Employee). In consideration of Employer's hiring Employee, Employee agrees as follows:

1. Agreement Not to Compete

While I, the Employee, am employed by Employer, and for two years afterward, I will not directly or indirectly participate in a business that is similar to a business now or later operated by Employer, in the same geographic area. This includes participating in my own business or as a co-owner, director, officer, consultant, independent contractor, employee or agent of another business.

In particular, I will not:

(a) Solicit or attempt to solicit any business or trade from Employer's actual or prospective customers or clients

(b) Employ or attempt to employ any employee of Employer

(c) Divert or attempt to divert business away from Employer, or

(d) Encourage any independent contractor or consultant to end a relationship with Employer.

Noncompete Agreement — Page 1 of 3

2. Right to an Injunction

I acknowledge and agree that if I breach or threaten to breach any of the terms of this agreement, Employer will sustain irreparable harm and will be entitled to obtain an injunction to stop any breach or threatened breach of this agreement.

3. Reasonableness

I acknowledge that the restrictions in this agreement are reasonable and necessary for the protection of Employer.

4. Survivability

This agreement will survive the termination, for any reason, of my employment with

5. Successors and Assignees

This agreement binds and benefits the heirs, successors and assignees of the parties.

6. Notices

All notices must be in writing. A notice may be delivered to a party at the address below or to a new address that a party designates in writing. A notice may be delivered:

Noncompete Agreement — Page 2 of 3

- in person

- by certified mail, or

- by overnight courier

Employer Address:

_____

Employee Address:

Address_____

City_____, Illinois

Zip Code_____

7. Governing Law

This agreement will be governed by and construed in accordance with the laws of the state of _____

Dated:

By:

Name _____

Disclaimer: This is not complete Form. Each State have different rules and regulations and when you obtain appropriate Form you need to indicate by which state law this is regulated. Best to consult your attorney. This Form is only a Sample. You can use this as an idea of incorporating this Form for protective practices in your business.

Noncompete Agreement — Page 3 of 3

Services not provided – Unless specifically agreed otherwise

Holidays:

As a general rule we do not work on holidays. The holidays we observe are:

- New Year's Day,
- Memorial Day,
- Independence Day,
- Labor Day,
- Thanksgiving Day and
- Christmas Day.

We contact our clients approximately two weeks before a holiday to arrange for an alternate date.

Health and Safety:

Staff are not allowed to climb any higher than a 2-step stool, move furniture that contains electronics or lift any objects over 20 pounds. Staff also do not prepare meals, do laundry, or provide any pet or children related services. Here is some advice for cleaners around issues pertaining to health and safety:

- Do not clean hazardously filthy homes or businesses.
- Do not clean any type of unsafe property.
- Do not clean unfinished/unsafe stairs.
- Avoid disaster cleaning post fire/water damage and smoke.

- Avoid ceiling and wall cleaning – Some homes do have at least one chandelier or vaulted ceiling van that cannot be reached by hand. We do offer chandelier cleaning as part of our window cleaning services.

- Do not move furniture but do your best to reach all visible places either by hand or with an extension duster.

- Avoid premises with unrestrained or unsupervised vicious pets.

- Do not clean out of your geographic area.

- Do not work for clients that treat you or other staff poorly.

- Do not let in other service/tradespeople such as water meter readers, UPS drivers and repair servicemen.

- If a house has old or damaged grout, only clean it and not repair it.

- Do not share any personal information from any client you have dealings with.

- We may limit or delay our services in extreme weather conditions such as a city or state declared emergency or unsafe working conditions.

- Cleaning is by appointment only. If you are unable to gain access to a home or you are turned away at the time of cleaning, there is a $50 service fee for that client.

Suggestions/Reminders to the client on the day you provide services.

On the scheduled day of your client's cleaning you could leave them this checklist:

- *Make sure your home is accessible to our employee /crew. Many of our customers provide us with keys.*

- *Make sure that your burglar alarm is turned OFF.*

- *Put away valuables and heirlooms etc. to avoid any accidents.*

- *Pick up after your pets and make sure they are secured.*

- *Make sure small children are not left alone to be exposed to cleaning supplies **as some products can be harmful if swallowed.***

Please give us a 48-hour notice if it is necessary to cancel or change your regular appointment.

If we receive less than 24-hour notice, or if upon arrival we cannot enter your home, it may be necessary to charge a $50 fee to cover our expenses.

Payment is due at the time of service, unless other arrangements are made.

If you forget to leave a check or make a payment during our cleaning visit, you still have an option to pay via PayPal or Credit Card.

*If you choose to pay by credit card, please know a **3%** surcharge will be added.*

Chapter 10

LEARNING HOW TO CLEAN

In this chapter you will learn the importance of getting your professional education in how to perform your services, to become the best in your industry.

There is a learning curve to performing professional cleaning services. Beginners need a little bit of guidance to help get your first paying clients and to hire your first employee. Everything else will become a repetition of what you have already done so far. With the advancement of Google, you are armed with a world of knowledge at your fingertips – and you will be able to avoid all my pre-Internet mistakes.

Cleaning people's homes it is a very personal business, a person-to-person industry, where happy clients refer their friends and family. When you conduct the job yourself, you are becoming your own boss in many ways. Cleaning services pay well, and you will be in control of your own hours. You will never look back on working for someone else.

If you need some extra money to help with the bills or pay a debt; cleaning can be the perfect in-between, permanent or full-time career. Startup costs are very low, and most people have the basic skills to start this business. However, don't leave this great opportunity to just basic skill, use your knowledge and drive to become an expert in the industry.

A good place to start its to concentrate on learning everything you possibly can about cleaning. Become a perfectionist! I could write entire chapters on cleaning methods but there is no point because this information is now easily obtainable online. Today you can use tutorials on everything – including how to resolve difficult cleaning tasks. You can now Google how to clean anything and YouTube tutorial videos show how to clean extremely tough or unique surfaces. There are also many books on how to clean, what supplies to use and tips and tricks to become an expert.

Soon you will see that the better quality of service you provide, the more clients you will get – and this can happen in a very short period of time. Your goal should be to have raving reviews from clients, to the point where they cannot even imagine how they did got so far without you, and I promise you, they will never leave!

Chapter 11

LOOKING PROFESSIONAL

In this chapter you will learn that you must look professional especially when on the job or estimating and performing cleaning services. This chapter also provides you with a few ideas about uniforms.

Your image will make or break the business. If you show up like you care less, your clients and your employees will care less too. It is best to have a cleaning company uniform that you always wear to work.

Part of looking professional is acting professionally. As discussed earlier, remember why you are there - to perform the professional service that you were hired to do. As part of your professional look it is also important to control your demeanor. Be focused, calm, friendly and pay attention to your client. Be confident and always follow up.

While on the first walkthrough of your clients' homes you will find out many important things that are impossible to learn other than by being present. Over the phone estimates or online forms should be only used to give your customer an idea of what you do and what you charge.

The walkthrough should be the final and bonding estimate, otherwise you may face problems down the road. If you do not have a walkthrough you may not fully understand the nature of the house you are cleaning. Your bid may be low, and you could be working too hard for too little money. Make sure to be attentive and listen to your client as much as possible.

I find it helpful to make notes and write down everything. These notes are important to make an estimate and compile a proposal. I also find it useful to not oversell yourself or your company; this is all about the client and what's in it for them.

Your potential client will tour you through their house, they will talk about people that live in the space and usually they will air their frustrations with previous cleaning services and you will get a feel of what is important to them. This information is gold, both for your proposal bid and for keeping them happy into the future.

Before you leave, just acknowledge that you are competent, qualified and accomplished.In my experience it is better to not give your client an estimate on the first visit, tell them you need to go to your office and calculate a great price for them. Tell them you will give them a detailed proposal to review.

If you see that there is price concern, tell them that you will come up with a way to save them on cleaning costs and that you will design a program that will be good for their home and save them in their back pocket.

You can ask them what they paid before. In many cases, they will tell you and you may discover that they paid more than you were going to charge them. Use this information wisely to charge them less than they paid before and more then you were going to charge them if you did not have this information. Everyone will be happy.

Please note if you **ever** feel uncomfortable at a house and you can spot potential danger for you or your crew, take this into consideration and decide carefully if you want to pursue this client.

Uniforms:

I found it useful to have 7 uniforms - one for every day of the week. Even if you are not working on a Sunday, you should always carry an extra one in the trunk just in case something unfortunate happens and you need to change your uniform while you are still working.

It is helpful to only launder once a week in preparation for a new week. Furthermore, choosing solid colors and a shirt with collar help create a professional and more elegant appearance. However, t-shirts and aprons in your company colors are also great. I like aprons, because they have so many useful pockets, which come in handy when you are cleaning.

When bidding on a job on location at client's house, I find it useful to wear more formal attire such as a polo shirt for a more professional appearance. Having pants of a solid color is also a useful tip, as it provides some continuity to the uniform. As well, pay attention to the fabric your uniforms are made from. Make sure they don't need ironing and once you choose your color, stick with it so you become consistently familiar to your clients and potential customers.

As far as footwear is concerned, tennis shoes are good choice and when inside your client's home you can use shoe covers that slide easily over your shoes. You can buy them in Wal-Mart, Menards or Home-Depot and they are inexpensive.

From a personal grooming perspective, make sure your breath is fresh, body is clean and free of odors or perfumes and your hair is well groomed or tied or pinned up. How people see you is how they project your company image. People form an opinion of you and your company, within the first few seconds. Remember that your prospective clients are no different. Based on their initial opinions of you they will make decision if they want to work with you or not. With this knowledge in mind you need to decide how you want to be remembered on your initial consultation.

Chapter 12

PRICING

In this chapter, we discuss pricing, the most sought-after tip in this industry. After reading this chapter you should gain an understanding and become comfortable with providing estimates to your clients and understand all the methods of pricing available to you depending on your niche/area. In addition, you will learn how to price for extras and the best way to offer your services.

There are two main methods for pricing a job:

1. Hourly rate

2. Price per square foot

Following the steps below will ensure the interview of your client for hiring your cleaning services goes smoothly.

The house itself is naturally the biggest factor in the weekly rate you charge for cleaning. The size, condition and maintenance of the home are other main factors that determine the time required to clean it. Additionally, clutter or numerous decorations make cleaning more difficult and time intensive. Some companies will request that picking up be done prior to their arrival to ensure their ability to clean an area.

I would recommend that you do the same for your company requirements. When talking to clients you can use this observation as one of few ideas on how to save them money on cleaning services. Also, this is one of the reminders that you can send to your clients, and we cover this in the chapter *Suggestions/Reminders* to the client.

Even the types of materials in the home, from appliances to flooring, can also change your time expectations for cleaning. A typical 2,000 square-foot home can take anywhere from three to six hours to clean depending on the makeup of the home. It helps to indicate to your clients the amount of time that you plan to spend in their home to give them a better idea of the expected thoroughness of your cleaning.

The type of residence may affect your cleaning service charge. Keep the following in mind and plan accordingly. These issues will affect the cleaning service final price:

- Condominiums and apartments are multi-unit dwellings. Your service may need special clearance to enter the building or complex.

- Town houses and duplexes usually have direct exterior entrances. However, parking may be an issue for your vehicle, especially if your client's home is part of a complex and located in the city - do you need to add the cost of parking?

- Some homes can be quite large and may be part of a gated community with an entrance pass. Do you need a code, or a card? Or do you need to wait for approval to enter?

- Does the house have antiques or other such items to be cleaned? Keep in mind it may cost more depending on how fragile they are, or if special cleaners or special cleaning equipment must be used.

When you set your appointment to see the house of a prospective client, remember what you are assessing. You are going there to assess the house for:

- Size,

- General cleanliness,

- How many people live in the house,

- How many bedrooms and bathrooms there are,

- How many pets; and most importantly

- What are the needs and wants of your client?

Finally, it is important to note whether you must pick up after your client? There is a joke about having to clean up before the maid arrives, but there is a reality behind it. If your client's teenage son has a bedroom full of clothing all over floor, it takes more time to hang, fold or bring it to the laundry room.

If your client's floor is cluttered or scattered with toys, books, games and so forth, it can be impossible to vacuum. If you agree to charge by the hour, then you might do it, but it's going to end up costing more for your client. Furthermore, very few people want to be responsible for breaking someone else's belongings. Try your utmost to make it your client's responsibility to pick up loose items before you arrive.

I mention in this book in the *Suggestions/Reminders* to your client chapter, about sending some gentle reminders to your client before your scheduled service via email or text. It is a good way to prompt your clients on what is helpful for you before their next clean.

Designated areas to be cleaned

It's a good idea to spend a few minutes to note which areas of home will be included in your scheduled cleaning service. If it is important to give certain areas special attention, make sure that your prospective client accepts your recommendations and in addition, agree that prior to each cleaning visit, they will leave a list of problem areas.

As noted earlier in this book, your professional appearance is important for your first impression. Make sure you are going to this meeting in your uniform, with your hair well- groomed and driving a clean car. It also helps to have all the essential forms that have been discussed including your *Client Information Form*, the *Pricing List*, the *Residential Bidding Form* and the *Menu* of services that you provide. And most importantly, be on time. Always be on time! Otherwise it won't matter what your pricing schedule looks like because your client simply will not hire you.

When it comes to pricing, provide your client with a price that is based on the estimated hours that will take to clean the entire house. Take into consideration how often the cleaning service will be provided. Whether a client accepts your proposal is going to come down to their budget and priorities. You may want to give your client a few options to choose from:

When meeting with your client it is important to give your client cleaning service options to choose from so they can get their house fully cleaned to the exact standards that they are after.

Here is a typical example you could present to your client regarding pricing:

- In my professional opinion, to clean all the rooms in this house with one or even two, **initial cleanings**, the charge would be $ __ea.

- Then, we recommend a **once a week cleaning service** for 5 hours. Not included in this proposal is changing the linen on all beds or making the beds. Alternatively, there is the following option:

- **Bi-weekly cleaning** for 6-8 hours and depending on what you agree as added services from our Menu. Additionally;

- **Once a month** additional service of (describe the area) for an additional price of $_____. (E.g., *Every last Friday of the month we will clean the inside of the refrigerator for an additional cost of $__.)*

From the walkthrough with your client make sure you have a draft of their final wishes. After this initial meeting it is then important that you go away and enter a formal proposal all you have agreed upon, describing exactly how often you will clean and what services are included in the package.

The next step is sending your proposal to your client, usually via email - make sure to include your proof of insurance. (See the list of items that you need to include in your proposal/agreement in the chapter *Useful Forms)*

Hourly Pricing

It is important to adjust your hourly rate as necessary, so that you remain competitive in your area. Depending on your business structure, the location of your services and the type of services you choose to provide, you can charge between $20-$45 per hour.

In the more affluent areas you can afford to charge on the higher side of this scale for your services. It is a good idea when you are starting out to charge less per hour, in order to get your full week of work and at the same time you can gain more experience to carry out excellent service.

At the earlier stages of your cleaning career, charging $20-$25 per hour will help you be very competitive. However, if you are charging a low price you must be mindful of your costs. You would rather ensure for this price that you are using your client's supplies and equipment and preferably working solo to reduce your overheads. If you provide additional labor, insurance and supervision, if you have other people working for you, logically you must charge more to remain profitable.

Charging per hour has its benefits. You will be paid per hour no matter how messy the house is and the hours that you stay working will determine your overall charge. Clients are more aware that if they do not pick up toys and clothing items off the floor, then your job will become more difficult and use more time to complete. As a result, clients usually do a superficial clean themselves and leave you to do the deeper cleaning. As an example, usually clients will empty the sink full of dirty dishes or remove clothing items from around the house and put away toys to help save you time.

If saving money is not the objective of your client, then usually the average house needs 6 to 8 hours to clean at $35 per hour.

If you work only 4 hours per day at the lowest charge of $25 per hour Monday - Friday, then the math is simple. You will make $500 per week. However, if you need more money to pay your bills of save for something, you may want to clean a house for 6 hours a day or a house for 4 hours and an additional apartment for 2 hours. That way you will make $750 a week before taxes.

Pricing Per Square Foot

Here is another few examples of prices for many common tasks and common extras that clients choose for their homes:

900 sq. ft. 2-bedroom apartment, 5 rooms:

One-time cleaning - **$80-$200**

Bi-weekly cleaning - **$60-$125**

1300 sq. ft. single-story home, 7 rooms:

One-time cleaning - **$100-$300**

Bi-weekly cleaning - **$85-$155**

2200 sq. ft. two-story 3-bedroom home, 9 rooms:

One-time cleaning - **$150-$400**

Bi-weekly cleaning - **$100-$180**

Extras:

Window cleaning, interior and exterior if safely possible-

$4-$7 per window

Refrigerator cleaning including removing and replacing items - **$35 - $80**

Oven cleaning - **$30-$60**

Move-in/move-out - **$160-$330**

If you see that your prospective client just got the sticker shock (they feel that the price is too high for them), then you can inform them that you have one opportunity for cleaning their house open for $100 or $150 on specific day from 8:AM - 12:PM or 8:AM-2:PM, and that you can start on your next available weekday.

By conversing with them in this manner you will make their decision easier and faster. By limiting your availability, you are essentially creating scarcity and stating that you have only one window of opportunity for them to hire you.

If they say that they would hire you, but the day you indicated is not good for them - ask them which day is workable and say that you will try to reschedule to accommodate them. In this instance say that you will call the next day to inform them if this is possible.

In addition, guarantee to 100% satisfy your clients when you perform your cleaning services. Make it clear if they are not 100% satisfied that you will come back the next day and make any corrections necessary until they are completely satisfied.

Chances are that with this approach you will land yourself a new client. Make sure not to fully close the window of opportunity on them and try to assure them that as soon as you have any availability you will call.

If the budget of your client is an issue, it can be prudent (while on a walkthrough) to suggest where they can save money. When you secure a client for your services you should hand them a list of things to do before you arrive. This list can contain a handful of suggestions and reminders to the client. Suggestions that save time and money for your clients will show them that you care for their expenses related to cleaning.

It is also particularly useful to create a list of the most frequently asked questions from clients, that you can provide answers. Include this information with your proposal/agreement package, or alternatively, send them to your website on which you should have a Q&A section available to view online or to be downloaded. Included at the end of this book is a Q&A of frequently asked questions, by clients, that you can use to provide your clients clarity.

A helpful list of additional services you can offer include:

- Interior Stove $30

- Interior of Oven $60

- Fridge $60

- Outside Windows

- Wiping Down Walls

- Garage cleaning

- Help at parties including cleaning dishes after party - $____ per hour

- Holiday charges - 50% more per hour

- Pet sitting while they on vacation

Move in/out cleaning

In this section we provide you with the estimated pricing rates for a move in /move out cleaning services. The move in/move out cleaning service is generally provided on a one-time only basis.

Prices are based per square foot of a home. Prices listed below are for vacant homes with utilities provided:

PLAN #1 (Minimum charge) up to 1,499 s.q. - **$180 + additional charge for windows inside $60.**

PLAN#2 - 1,500 - 1,999 sq. ft. - **$220 + additional charge for windows inside $90.**

PLAN #3 - 2,000 - 2,499 sq. ft. - **$250 + additional charge for windows inside $120.**

PLAN #4 - 2,500 - 2,999 s.q. f.t. - **$280 + additional charge for windows inside $140.**

PLAN #5 - 3,000 - 3,499 sq. ft. - **$320 + additional charge for windows inside $180**

PLAN #6 - 3,500 - 3,999 s.q. f.t. - **$380 + additional charge for windows inside $220**

PLAN #7 - 4,000 sq. Ft and up - **10 cents** per s.q. f.t.

All trash-outs are individually priced as each project differs.

Chapter 13

FORMS OF PAYMENT

In this chapter you will learn about your options to be paid. Also included are suggestions for remedies in situations of non-payment from your clients.

In your contract you will indicate the form of payment you wish to receive. If you don't have a PayPal account yet, now is the time to get one. Once you have your business checking account and e-mail account, you will be ready to set-up a free PayPal account to accept credit cards online.

www.paypall.com

When it comes to housekeeping, it is wise for your business to make payment due at the time of service. Clients have the option of payment by credit card Visa, MasterCard, Discover (if you choose to set it up), check or cash. Make it clear to clients if they choose to pay by credit card that a 3% surcharge will be added.

When you agree on a day and time of service, you need to inform your client that you accept checks or cash and the client is not home, that they can leave it on their kitchen counter and you will pick their payment up after you finish cleaning. It is helpful to tell your clients that this is the most popular method of payment. In addition, inform them that you accept Visa, Credit Cards and PayPal and you are happy to accept the form of payment that is easier for them to use. Mostly, in my experience, you receive checks.

If for some reason they have not left a payment for you and no-one is going to show up before you leave, then you should leave a note with your company name and information of non-payment and suggest that they can pay by PayPal when they return from work.

If you don't get any payment on that same day, you should issue an Invoice.

Occasionally you will face circumstances where the client does not pay. What are your options if the client did not respond to your note or invoice and you already sent a reminder about the scheduled cleaning service. Or the next day you show up on the job and there is no check to make up for last week or for today's work?

In my experience it is best to try and communicate with the client at the earliest possible stage. Try to call, and if there is no answer? I would not perform the service this day; instead I would leave a note (you have seen this previously in *Useful Forms*): *Your Company Name*

Address

E-mail

Phone number

Today's Date

Dear Client,

I have shown up for work today and see that you did not leave a check for your last cleaning that I performed on _____ day, I hope it's not because you are not happy with my performance. If you are, please let me know.

Just in case that you may be unhappy with my service, I do not want to continue and make you disappointed again. Therefore, I did not clean today. Please note that you are liable for the non-payment and non-cancellation of services charged to the amount of $50.

Please contact me at your earliest convenience to remedy this situation, or to cancel your services, as per our agreement, dated _____.

Sincerely,

Your name_____

Chapter 14

HOW TO LAND YOUR FIRST CLIENT

In this chapter you will learn successful methods that you can use to land and retain your first clients

Finding your first clients can be as basic as putting flyers in apartment buildings, local stores and mailboxes in the neighborhood where you want to work.

Concentrating on working in one area of your city saves you time and gas money, so it may be worthwhile to offer discounts to those who are close to your home, or alternatively, to charge higher rates to those who are further away.

People start cleaning businesses all the time and the competition can be fierce. Do not let this deter you from starting your own service. Maid and cleaning services are only as reputable and popular as their attention to quality and detail, in addition to the fair price.

Your job is to be better than your competition and providing the best cleaning service is fundamental to your success.

If you want to work solo - for this business model it is not necessary to create a website, instead here are some suggestions:

- Announce your new cleaning service business opening at your desired by printing a flyer. This flyer should contain information that you are new in the area and are now offering your cleaning services with a promotional price of $x. Make sure you have determined the geographical area of your services. The less distance you must travel the lower your costs are.

- When you get a new client, introduce yourself to the neighbors and give them your business card. Create a business card that displays your logo, your company name, address, e-mail, and your name and phone number. Your logo helps with credibility and makes you look like a real business. Make sure your logo quickly and clearly identifies what you do.

- On the reverse side of your business card don't miss the opportunity to use this advertising space and indicate which cleaning services you provide and what discount you can offer for a first-time service request. (It helps to leave the amount of your discount blank to be filled out by hand, so you can adjust it as necessary). It can also be helpful to have an expiry date on your first-time deals as that works as a call to action for your clients.

- Print flyers and hand deliver them – in my experience do not leave a flyer in the mailbox, unless you paid postage. Leave them in prospective client's newspaper slot if they have it, or print a door hanger flyer and hang them on their door.

- Install a calendar on your smartphone to make sure that you can schedule all your requests for cleaning, or use Pocket Suite, www.pocketsuit.io

- Make sure you send confirmation 24 hours before your scheduled arrival.

- It can also be helpful to advertise in local community papers, churches and other weekly newsletters and publications.

- Make use of local companies that send the online coupons *Groupon,* it will cost about $125 if they have a discount from you for your services. Make sure your coupons are for services for new clients only, or on specific days of the week. Be very specific on the coupons and indicate precisely how they can be used. Also, be wary that too many coupons are unhelpful, and you may want to only make 20 coupons available.

Always ask how the client found you, so you can determine what form of advertising is working for you and what's not.

It is also vital to **ask for referrals** from your happy clients. Let them know that you have one cleaning window open and are looking for more work if they know of anyone to recommend that would be great. Always be very positive, happy and appreciative of the work that you have with them. Offer them a free hour or two, depending on the quality of the referral.

Almost every neighborhood these days has their own Facebook groups or next-door sites that people use to refer service trades to each other. If your client advertises your services on these forums, you may gain several service requests. Your referral fee may gain a much higher value than the 2 free hours of service you offer in return.

When I started my first business I was buying customer contacts from those who were leaving the country and from various Employment Agencies. Nowadays, you can accomplish the same feat by creating a landing page for your business, or your company website, if you want to expand your business and hire other people to work for you.

Chapter 15

TRANSITION FROM WORKING SOLO TO AN OWNER/OPERATOR

In this chapter you will learn how to set up a business model to grow – and how to replace yourself from the cleaning solo business model.

Transition Steps to grow your business

This is to give you an idea how the actual transition works and how to step away from the cleaning solo business model. We will cover more on growing your business in the *Magnetic Marketing* chapter of the book.

When you work solo, there is no need to make a payroll for yourself. You will not pay self-employment taxes. All proceeds are going to your personal account.

There is no need to make a special bank account. Simply add your name to an existing account to get your checks cashed. Just don't forget to have separate accounting for your deductible business expenses.

When choosing your business name, make it easy to pronounce. My first residential cleaning service company was Teresa's Cleaning Service. If I knew then, what I know now, I would choose less personal name for my company. I thought this will be easier to remember, but I never thought of future selling the business and loss of value because of it. Make it easier to remember in some other way, because by making it easier to remember it becomes easier to find you. When you decide on your company name, then from this point, you can create an email account with the name of your business and use it for your PayPal account as a paying option.

The ultimate goal, as you transition your business, is to create next level growth. Starting solo and scaling your business for the future is a must. Learn the process to obtain enough clients, so you can hire your next person and so on, until your business grows to a point that you become a Manager of Operations and later, a President of your company - with people working for you in the field, as well as in the office.

In the beginning, once you have two apartments, two small homes or one large home to clean for the same day, I recommend start taking your future employee with you for training, while at the same time helping you to share the workload.

Soon you will have 2 requests for every working day in the week for your new hire. *Refer to the Case Study.* Now prepare for the next person by filling your own schedule to full capacity and repeat the process.

Your business growth is tied up to your company's reputation. Become a pro in hiring new people, training them and checking on their performance. This is the best way to replace yourself in the business gradually with another capable person.

Hiring additional personnel is especially beneficial for you when you need a day off or time away from the job because of illness or a need for a vacation. Most importantly in this situation you don't want your business to stop when you are not around.

Another good idea is to hire another person for an on-call position that you can use for emergency situations.

Solutions for sick day or vacations

When you or your employees get sick or are need vacation, it is vital to replace them for all their regular scheduled and repeat clients.

In my experience, the best way to solve this problem is to send a group of two or three employees along to complete the jobs, where the regular person is unavailable, ideally with you being one of them. This solution makes sure the client remains happy even though you are changing personnel.

From my experience, clients become very attached to the person that comes to clean their home on a regular basis. They view it as a bit of a problem when they see someone new at their home. But if you are part of the crew, they will feel secure and appreciative that you really care for them.

When your business grows bigger, you will ideally have a quality control manager that comes from time to time to each client's homes to check if all that you promised the client is being delivered and that the quality of service remains at the high standard you set in the beginning. Then, in this case, your clients will get used to dealing with the manager and if someone is sick, they will be in position to step in and be one of the crew-members.

In a situation where you must change personnel for a client's residence, it is important that you temporarily fill the void to maintain some form of familiarity for your client. This way you can also train the new hire and ensure the clean is carried out effectively. When your business grows sufficiently your quality control manager should step into your shoes and train the new hire. This makes the transition smooth for the client and is an effective way to keep all your business.

Chapter 16

HIRING AND TRAINING YOUR WORKERS

In this chapter you will learn the importance of training your employees and how to create the reasons why someone would like to work for you.

When you hire new people, you want to make sure that they are going to reflect well on your company. For this reason, it is imperative to drug screen and background check your prospective staff. But most importantly, your staff must be properly trained to clean your client's homes without your supervision.

I like to stress the importance of training because this will make or break your business and future growth.

Just remember that going to clean other people's homes require knowledge on how to perform cleaning to the professional standard that your business sets. You must teach your new hires what solutions to use on which surface - because not knowing this may create a lot of liability issues for you down the track. For example, if you use oven spray on furniture it can have disastrous consequences. It can happen because the spray cans for cleaning these surfaces are very similar in appearance.

It is important to receive ongoing education of what is now available in the market to solve problems. Then you will be able to relay this information to your employees.

Appearance is also important. To assure that your people will represent you properly, you need to be an example and train them effectively. Even during the training period, the use of uniforms is very important.

Always make sure that your new hires are performing their services up to your company standards and to the specific needs of your clients. By far, the best training technique is hands on experience, with you, on location. It involves longer hours, but you are training your hire specifically for the location that they will work at later.

With today's technology, many clients will have outside and inside cameras as part of their security system. Make sure you and your staff are used to the idea that you may be on the camera. Camera or not, work and act as if you were on the camera at all times. It is also important to train your staff to always be on time for your scheduled cleaning visit.

It is important to have all your liability and administration sorted before you take a new hire on location for training. Don't ever take a person with you, on any account, if this person is not covered by your insurance - workers compensation, liability insurance and bonding. This is a protective business expense. Make sure that all parties involved will be protected - you, your worker and the client. Besides, your business will be so much more valuable to your client when you send a proposal or contract for cleaning with the proof of insurance attached.

Invest necessary time and effort to give your potential hires good training and remember about the importance of ongoing training, especially for your newer staff. This will repay itself in the future, providing that they continue working with you.

Retention of staff is an important point to consider in any business. To make sure that your employees are staying with you, it is vital you become very aware of the treatment of your staff. Treat your employees with respect and appreciation and they will become dedicated employees. A good method to use is to create a rewards system and always be on the lookout for those employees that you can promote to Field Manager.

Show your staff appreciation for what they are doing right. Then they will strive to do their best for you and your company. Once you have this rapport in place with your staff and you trust them to work independently, you can take that one-day of the week and use that time to look for more clients and hire more superstar employees.

Now is the time to become a leader. Becoming a leader is so much different to becoming a manager. Managers are influencing things in a single moment. Conversely, a leader is somebody with a vision that influences others in such way that they follow their vision willingly. Every team, no matter how small, needs a leader, whether they are appointed or not. People are looking for and crave leadership.

Are you that person?

You must master the skills of leadership and become an extraordinary influencer.

In my experience there are three levels of leadership:

- **1st level** - when you can influence yourself to do something to make a change that makes a significant difference in your life.

- **2nd level** – is when you influence and teach another person how to significantly change things in their lives.

Teaching them the steps that they can take in order to positively change their behavior, motivate them and give them your knowledge.

- **3rd level** - is when you can teach and influence a group of people to make a shift, to motivate them to action, share your knowledge to change their life, behaviors and awareness.

Become a leader in your own company.

Chapter 17

WHY SHOULD CLIENTS CHOOSE YOU?

In this chapter we examine what you can do as a business leader to ensure that people continually turn to your business to provide them with exceptional cleaning services.

An informed client will interview several cleaning services before choosing one. They will ask for references and check them. After all, you will be spending time in their home. They must be comfortable with you and vice versa. Trust is very important, since the cleaner(s) will have access to your client's entire house.

Who is your competition?

There are many cleaning services and maid services to choose from. They range from individual people looking for extra income, to local boutique companies and fully-fledged corporations with nationwide services and franchises.

Independent operators – often they charge less, sometimes as little as $15 an hour. Independents can sometimes negotiate an acceptable rate. Few, if any, will require a contract and most can easily accommodate changes to their cleaning schedule. Many can provide references to attest to the quality of their work and to their personal integrity and honesty. They usually don't provide insurance or bonding.

Maid service companies – they are bonded, licensed and insured, but they usually cost more, around $25 to $45 per person, per hour or more. Many require contracts and may or may not be able to accommodate last-minute schedule changes. However, maid service companies have better dependability. If one of the maids is out sick, they can call in another employee who will have the same qualifications to adapt to the needs of the client and keep the schedule.

Why should a client hire your company instead of any other company or individual?

This is what has worked for my cleaning businesses and will work for you:

- Pride yourself on your dedication and your excellence, because your client deserves the best!

- Guarantee the 100% satisfaction of your client. *'We guarantee that you will be happy with the quality of our service, or we will return the next day and clean it again at no additional cost!'*

- Tailor your service to meet the needs of your client.

- Ensure your staff are highly trained, professional, dependable and courteous.

- Be fully insured and bonded.

- Conduct state and nationwide criminal background checks on all employees.

- Be locally and independently owned, not a franchise.

- Quality control – quality should be your number one priority. Ensure that you have a quality control manager to check on performance.

- While checking on performance, your quality control manager should provide feedback on the quality of service performed by your staff. They should also provide reminders/suggestions on things that you would like to be improved.

- It can be helpful to perform random surveys by calling customers to check on the quality of work, to ensure the level of service is exemplary. Remember, you want your clients to be 100% satisfied.

- Go above and beyond. If someone in your client's household has allergies or specific needs, do everything in your power to assist by purchasing specific products that will be beneficial for them, even if they are not necessarily available to the general public.

Here are some other ideas on why potential clients and customers should choose you:

'There's no risk in choosing us! We are not a franchise company. We are a local boutique cleaning service that is dedicated to totally satisfying our clients. We treat your home like our own! Learn more about our 100% satisfaction guarantee.'

When you experience **no sales** for your services, you need to revisit certain facts:

- Is your service needed in this specific market?

- Are your prices right for this market?

- Do you need to change the services that you providing?

- Do you need to change the prices to make the sale?

- Should you change your method of promotion?

If you choose to advertise your services online – be it via website, social media, or any other form of online marketing, you need to create informative messaging:

- What does your business do?

- How does it improve your client's life?

- How are you different from your competition?

- Give them a reason why they should choose you.

- Tell them where you operate

A great way to think about your marketing is like this:

What would your business be like if it was perfect? Keep seeking out ways on how your service can become better and better. This is a good idea to keep in mind when you first create your:

- **Company logo** – It is quite inexpensive these days to create a logo. You can create one easily by simply searching 'logo contests' on Google, or go to www.48hourslogo.com, www.99design.com, www.fiverr.com, www.vistaprint.com and many more. There are so many sites available where you can create your own logo, business cards, flyers and a whole host of other marketing materials.

- **Business cards** – They can help dramatically with your credibility when you first introduce your company to prospective clients.

- **Uniforms** – Think about what you want to display by having a uniform. Your logo and your company name are a good starting point. Looking professional can make the world of difference in this industry.

- **Your appearance and persona** – The way you speak, the way you look and the people who represent you are all critical factors in marketing.

- **Other marketing materials** – It helps to have consistency with things such as your invoices, worksheets, the description of your services, the terms of your service and payment methods.

- **Landing page/Website** – Online content is so important in our modern society and this trend is only going to increase.

Chapter 18

BRANDING

In this chapter you will learn the importance of branding from the very start of your business.

These lessons are what I learned from Small Business Administration. I discovered a few things relevant to branding that will be beneficial for your cleaning venture:

Branding – Your brand is your promise to your customer. It explains and details what they can expect from your service and how you are different from your competition.

Branding is one of the most important aspects of any business, large or small. An effective brand strategy gives you a major edge in an increasingly competitive market.

Your brand comes from who you are, who you want to be and who people perceive you to be.

Is your service a high-cost, high-quality option? Or is your business a low-cost, high-value option? Who you become should be based, to some extent, on your target market.

The foundation of your brand is your logo. Your website and promotional materials, all should integrate your logo and it should communicate your brand effectively.

Brand strategy – Your brand strategy is the how, what, where, when and to whom you plan on communicating and delivering your brand messages. Where you advertise is part of your brand strategy. Your distribution channels are also part of your brand strategy. Also, what you communicate visually and verbally to your potential customers are part of your brand strategy. Remember, the added value to your customers comes frequently in the form of perceived quality, or in the form of emotional attachment. Therefore, your reputation as a business is so important.

Defining your brand – Defining your brand requires, at the very least, that you answer these questions below:

- What is your company's mission? A very simple mission statement can be:

'My mission is to be the very best at what I am doing'; or

'My mission is to become the best quality service in my market'.

- What are the benefits and features of your service?

- Why and how are you different?

- What is your area of specialization in your industry? Some suggestions of specialization include cleaning homes after construction, move in/move out services, window cleaning, pressure washing, apartments only, residences only, chandelier cleaning etc., etc.

- What do your prospective and existing customers think of your company?

- What is your competitive advantage? (What do you do better than everybody else in the market)

- In what way is the service you offer superior?

- What qualities do you want your customers to associate with your company?

Once you have defined your brand, it is imperative to get the word out about your business. Here are a few time-tested tips to help you get your brand out in the open:

1. Find a unique name – Create a memorable name for your company.

2. Get a great logo – And place it everywhere.

3. Write down your brand messaging – What are the key messages you want to convey about your brand? Every employee should be aware of the key attributes of your brand.

4. Integrate your brand - Branding extends to every aspect of your business- how you answer your phones, what you or your staff wear on sales calls, your e-mail signature, everything.

5. Develop a tagline - Write a memorable, meaningful and concise statement that captures the essence of your brand.

6. Design marketing materials - Use the same color scheme, logo placement, and look and feel throughout. You don't need to be fancy, just consistent.

7. Be true to your brand - Customers won't return to you or refer you to someone else if you don't deliver on what your brand promises.

8. Be consistent - This is the most important tip. If you can't do this, your attempts at establishing your brand will fail.

Example of Branding I

Imagine that a prospective customer is calling you over with an intention to hire your services and they want to meet you and talk to you. When you arrive, you enter in to the living room, and see four people there, representing your competition. The prospective client tells you that they will hire one of you and they have more work to give you. But first, they want to ask you one question - and whatever answer you give - he wants your competitor do not disagree with your statement, and say-*"No you are not"*.

The question is: *What can you do better than your competitors?*

Maybe you can say you are accommodating your clients with the greatest speed, or you have the best customer service, or maybe you have the best prices. It could even be that you have a 100% quality guarantee, or it is free.

Your competitors, whatever they will say, they should not argue that - *"this statement is not true because ......"!*

What would your answer be? What is your unique selling proposition? It must be something that no one in your market is offering. Sometimes your distinct selling proposition exists because of you. How do you provide your service in your style, better than anybody else?

Example of Branding II

Picture yourself that you are hiring a cleaning service for your investment of several apartment buildings in the area. Your offer is very appealing it will require two people, five days per week, full time position. If this work out, you will hire them to work for you on 4 additional locations, that need accommodate very soon.

You have invited four companies to your office to present your specifications.

Now that you have already talk to them, received their proposals, you have to make decision who to hire.

On what basis you will make your decision?

Will you make your decision based on their appearance, their knowledge and experience, eagerness to get the job, price?

What do you think your decision would be?

If you don't have a competitive advantage yet, you need to develop it now!

Make it at least in one area of your core business.

Create a branding video

If you can create a branding video that you can upload to YouTube, you are well on your way to conveying your branding message to your prospective customers.

One of the things I've found is that many entrepreneurs and small business owners have huge difficulty articulating what they actually do. Here is my formula for crafting a marketing message to attract your ideal client:

1. You need to identify your ideal client. Who are they?

2. Learn the needs, habits and desires of your current and prospective customers. Don't assume what they think, know and what they desire.

3. Create an-avatar or a profile of your ideal client. If you have already started a business, think about your best clients that you work with now or have in the past:

- What are they like?

- What attributes do they have?

- Can you describe them?

- Can you give them a name?

- What are their pain points?

- What are their fears, frustrations, challenges and doubts?

- What do they want and need?

- What do they desire?

- How old are they?

- Where do they live and work?

- How much money do they earn?

- Can they afford your services?

Spend some time on this because you will use this to craft your message.

4. What credibility and authority do you have for doing what you do? Is it the length of time you have been in business or your experience?

5. What is your offer or invitation; and finally,

6. What is your promise?

Now that you have all this information, put it together and edit it so that it takes no more than 1-5 minutes to say. This easily becomes your script for your Personal Branding Video.

Chapter 19

MAGNETIC MARKETING

In this chapter I will show you that marketing is all about getting your name out there and attracting customers. It is then your responsibility to let them know the value you bring. If you don't tell them your value - they will never know what you are worth!

Your ability to market effectively is the most important single business skill you can develop. If you want to make a lot of money, be successful, prosperous and retire financially independent - you absolutely must market effectively. Marketing is the key to business success in any economic situation. Simply put, marketing is your key to more sales. Before you start, determine your target clientele and identify their expectations. As we covered in the previous chapter on *Branding*, it is important to create a company image that will attract customers.

Make sure you note the following points in ***Gold!*** The importance of this information cannot be underestimated:

Everything you do to merchandise your cleaning service including your website, printing, advertising and anything else - try to dig inside your client's mind.

Ask your customers what they are looking for in a cleaning service? What are they not getting, or lacking right now? Listen to the exact words that they are using. Find out what their problems are and understand them even better than they do. Position yourself to be able to say, '*I have a solution to meet your needs*'.

Here is an example of an interaction with a potential client that will help explain the magnetic marketing principles with clarity. Whether you call people or talk to them in person ask them the following:

'*I have question for you; I am looking for people that have used cleaning service companies in the past. I want to be the #1 provider of cleaning services in my industry, so I need your help:*

1. What do you love about their services?

2. What do you dislike?

3. What would you change about them so that a cleaning service could better accommodate your needs?'

Amazing service sells itself!

No matter what state the economy is in, there are always going to be more people to sell services than people to buy them. As a result, customers are going to have to choose from different services that are available, and your job is to make sure that they choose you.

Your ability to enter into and succeed in a competitive market determines your sales, your growth, your profitability and your long-term success.

The purpose of marketing is to make selling unnecessary

How is this even possible? At its very least, effective marketing should make selling easy. Marketing should differentiate your service from your competitors. The purpose of marketing is to claim things, show things, prove things and illustrate things to show that what you are selling is superior and differentiated from your competition.

There is only one reason that people buy anything and that is to improve their lives or their work in some way. When you define your business, it should be in terms of what your service can do for others. How does your cleaning improve the life or the work of your client's? How can you achieve this for them in a cost-effective way?

What people really buy is how they feel as a result using your service. How will your clients feel if they accept your services? Will they feel happier, more comfortable, more relaxed, richer, more respected, more admired? It is important to tap into the emotional ingredients that are responsible for 80% of the decision-making that goes into to using your services.

Who is your ideal customer? If you would run an advertisement for a perfect customer in your local paper, what would you say in that advertisement? Here is an idea:

'Perfect Client Wanted! They must own a house in __ neighborhood. They must earn a minimum of $__ per year. They must be working and too busy to clean the house. They must require cleaning services at least __ times a month.'

Now you should be able to easily imagine your ideal client and start looking for them.

The quality of your service has two parts to it. It's the service itself and how the service was delivered. In my experience, only 20% is the actual service and 80% of it is the way you treat people. This is important at every single stage of your business interactions with your clients. From the very first phone call through to the last communication of the sale; every instant of customer contact is the moment of truth. It is these interactions that show the customer why they should use your services repeatedly and why they should refer you to their friends.

Make sure that your services do what you say they will do and continues to do so.

In other words, make sure that your service fulfills what you promised.

Create the processes from the very beginning and simplify your business life. It will be very easy to follow when you start to hire employees. Keep documentation of everything so you can give this to a new hire and explain things clearly to your staff if they are unsure about it. Your documented instructions will become a reference point.

You can create instructions on how to answer a call - follow a script until you know it by heart. You can do the same with how to respond to emails and address issues in various situations - add them to your documentation library and develop them as your business operations grow in time.

Advertising/Marketing

Advertising and marketing are important aspects to starting any business, especially for a cleaning service run from home.

Here are some house cleaning ads that have worked for me in my businesses:

- **Advertise in your local paper or online on your local websites**: A simple text ad under the 'services offered' in your local paper or weekly rag is a good start. Make it short and simple. Something as simple as, *'Housecleaning, please call Teresa at 111-1111'* can be effective. It also pays to check what they will charge to run an ad on the online versions of these papers.

- **Flyers**: Creating a flyer is a great way to advertise/market your services. It can even be hand-written; if necessary, you just make sure it is neat. By folding it in half and taping it closed, you can send it to local homes through the mail. This way you will not get in trouble leaving them at the mailbox without postage. Depending on your area, you might even be able to go door to door in neighborhoods that you would like to work in and pass out your flyers. Depending on your local laws, you also may be able to personally hand them to the homeowner or put them on or in the front door, or in their newspaper mailboxes if they have them. It is also a good idea to hang them on public bulletin boards.

- **Business Cards**: Another good marketing tool you can print your own are business cards. There are also several online sites as well as office supply stores where you can get simple business cards printed inexpensively. Have some printed with your name, the type of cleaning service you perform and your phone number. (Refer to this in the *Getting Your First Clients* chapter).

- **References that you can provide**: References are a great tool to spread your business by word of mouth. Your first references can come from those people who are willing to give you a good name. Ask friends that you have known for a while if they would be keen to do that for you. Then, in any advertisement you create, make sure to mention that you have references and give them to any prospective customers who ask. As you start cleaning one or two houses and make your clients happy with your quality of performance, ask those customers if you can use them as references also. I used to give customers a discount or a free cleaning if they referred a friend. You can even advertise that that you give discount for referrals in your flyers or business cards.

Samples of advertising:

This one I sent to apartment complexes in my area:

1. *(Your Co. name) _____ is not just for those who are looking for a weekly clean. If you are moving out of your apartment, make sure you get your entire security deposit back and schedule a cleaning with some added extras to leave the place spotless. Or maybe you just signed a new lease and want someone to do a deep clean before you move in. We would like to become your cleaning service provider. Whether you are looking for a house clean, apartment clean, regular or deep clean, move-in or move-out cleaning – we do it all!*

2. *We at (your Co. name) help return your bedrooms, bathrooms, kitchen, living room and more to the as new condition that you remember from when you first moved in!*

Chapter 20

YOUR WEBSITE CONTENT

This chapter will show you how easy it is to get your own website - a virtual home for your business with windows to the world. Discover how to create your own business website, as well as learn from many examples of the type of content you may want to include on your pages.

Your website is your first step towards a professional appearance in the eyes of your clients. In my experience, your website message should be 80% about your visitor and 20% about your services and offerings. Focus on your customers and list all the benefits that they receive when they hire you. Recognize what their problems are and show them how you have the solution.

Imagine that you are looking for a cleaning service just like yours. What would you like to see on the website that you visit? When creating your website and web content, always remember the voice of your client, *'what's in it for me?'* Then tell them how they will benefit from hiring you. It is important to effectively use a call to action button so that your website becomes your own digital calling card.

To create a website, you will need:

A Website Template

You can buy your own template for website very inexpensively. Examples are https://webmonsters.com, https://envatoelements.com . Buying your website will assure that you own a license for this template. The WordPress format is very easy to navigate and great for making changes.

A Hosting Platform

These cost about $150 a year. GoDaddy.com or Hostgater.com are a good place to start.

A Domain Name

Depending on the name of your business and if it is available, this can cost from as little as $10.

Website Integration

Your website can and should be integrated with social media channels. Just to give your idea how much it could cost you to create a simple website, the latest quote that I got on my most recent website was between $500-$1500.

Website Content

Create content for your website or hire a writer by giving them a rough draft of what you want your pages to look like. www.upwork.com, www.freelancer.com and www.ewriters.com are all great freelance websites where you can turn your scribbling into masterpieces. Before you hire someone, it helps to know what your website should look like so you can give your writer some great ideas.

Imaging

We are all visual creatures, so you are going to need some pictures for your website. You can buy stock photos from various website destination like www.deposit-photos.com, and www.photos.com. Another inexpensive idea that you can play with in your own time is to create your own photo session at your client's home. If you follow this route it can be a good idea to offer a free cleaning service in exchange for being able to get a photo shoot. Make sure they sign a release agreement, so you can use the photos on your website.

Hire IT help

There are several questions that you will probably have that you need to ask your IT specialist. Here are some common questions:

- How long does it take to create a website? In my experience, depending on their work schedule, it can usually be completed in a week.

- How much will it cost you to make your website live and operating?

- What is the on-going management cost?

- What is the cost of future updates? Usually it is calculated at a cost per hour.

Suggestions on what you can use as your website content

Include your service area:

A good starting point is to include your geographical service area on a Google map. An example of the content that can go with this map could be as follows:

'For your convenience, a map of our service area and list of zip codes is posted below. If you click on the map, you will get an enlarged image. If you have any questions as to whether we service your home, please call or email us at ___.'

Or,

'Map with your cleaning area indicated here'

Or,

'Areas served - We are providing the highest-level cleaning services in your city and in your local neighborhood.' (Followed by a list of neighborhoods that you are servicing)

Call to Action:

A call to action button is a way to entice potential customers to utilize your services. This button could be accompanied by text such as:

'Click here to schedule'

'Make reservation here'

'Schedule cleaning'

'Request free proposal'

'Check for availability'

Install a calendar:

If people can access your schedule and check your availability, they are more likely to place a reservation with you. You will be informed via email, or text about your new request.

There are many online calendars that you can use, and the *Google calendar* is a great place to start. Train yourself to set your schedule availability and check and confirm appointments as they come. You can set the system to send you automatic reminders and it can also send them to your clients.

I recommend scheduling your client appointments on an elegant work calendar and you can then sync it with your Google calendar to set appointment reminders and even integrate online booking.

Booking options:

Booking can also can be done on your smartphone, or website, or both - using Pocket Suite www.pocketsuite.io. It will take care your basic needs of running your residential cleaning service. You can choose between the free and paid version of this software. Using this software, you can select low processing as one of the methods of payments.

Booking online is very convenient, but you need to make sure that your calendar is reflecting your true availability and is maintained regularly and kept up to date.

Invoicing:

Send professional invoices to clients. Deliver invoices via text message or email and allow clients to conveniently pay online via your website.

Messaging:

Send instant messages to your clients via SMS text. Get a unique phone number for your business and keep all customer communication in an organized feed.

Payments:

Link a checking account and receive a direct deposit for any client credit card payments. Allow clients to pay online or use a simple point-of-sale to charge cards, where you should charge a flat processing fee (usually 2.7-3.0%) and with a 1-2-day direct deposit.

More ideas for content:

Here is an example of content for a flyer you can use to distribute to your potential clients:

The most (desirable/convenient/affordable) name in home cleaning,

Do you need to prepare your home for viewing by potential buyers?

Here's how it works, just go to our website (insert website) and schedule a date on our calendar. Tell us your zip code and how big your home is. Then we will call you to confirm our visit and give you a free estimate. We will provide you with professional cleaning services to help you gain more time and take away the stress of cleaning your home.

You may want to set-up your website in such a way that after your client visits your website and clicks on a certain call to action such as *'instant estimated pricing'*, clients will be able to insert information about their home such as its size, the frequency of cleaning they require, their zip code, their location and their desired date of cleaning. It can be helpful to have an hourly rate associated with your services, which can act as an estimate for your clients.

Here are a few additional examples of prices for many common tasks and some extras:

900 sq. ft. 2-bedroom apartment, 5 rooms:

- One-time cleaning - **$80-$200**

- Bi-weekly cleaning - **$60-$12**

1300 sq. ft. single-story home, 7 rooms:

- One-time cleaning - **$100-$300**

- Bi-weekly cleaning - **$85-$155**

2200 sq. ft. two-story 3-bedroom home, 9 rooms

- One-time cleaning - **$150-$400**

- Bi-weekly cleaning - **$100-$180**

Window cleaning, interior (exterior if safely possible) - **$4-$7 per window**

Refrigerator cleaning (including removing and replacing items) - **$35 - $80**

Oven cleaning - **$30-$60**

Move-in/move-out - **$160-$330**

You have to ensure that your clients understand that these prices are **only an estimate** and the final price needs to be confirmed after viewing their home. The price is also contingent on the cleanliness of the premises. As an example, you can give this explanation:

'If you choose regular cleaning and your house, in fact, needs a deep clean, then our price will change accordingly. Instant pricing is just to give you an idea how much it may cost if your evaluation is correct.'

Should you hire a weekly, bi-weekly or monthly cleaner?

To decide how often you have a cleaning service come to your home depends on your needs, your schedule and your budget. You might need just a little help staying on top of things. Maybe you are a little older or a student, or you might just need help because of your busy schedule. Or maybe, you just want to impress your guests that you frequently entertain.

Here is an idea of what the various schedules we offer:

- ***Weekly****: A weekly clean is ideal for those with busy lives and lots of social obligations. For these people, even a* *simple wiping down of kitchen cabinets, counters and vacuuming can put a crimp in their overloaded schedules. Even those who work at home or stay at home with children can find themselves without the time to do much beyond the bare necessities depending on the nature of the work.*

- *Bi-weekly: As a general up-keep type of service, this is the most popular schedule for many homes. It is ideal for someone who is busy, but not overloaded with work or social commitments.*

- *Monthly: A once a month thorough clean provides a good, regular service for your home. While it can be costlier than the previous two options - because of the workload involved - it is also often a popular option for those with a minimalist lifestyle and who may not have particularly loaded schedules.*

Usually, the more often a cleaning service comes out to your house, the less it will cost you per visit. Weekly and bi-weekly visits are not only more cost effective; they're also healthier for you. A routine clean of your home reduces allergens, bacteria, and other health concerns for your family.

After reviewing your home, we will provide you with a free in-home estimate of each of your service options, so that you know exactly what to expect moving forward.

Our Guarantee

If for any reason you are not 100% satisfied with our home cleaning service, we ask that you let us know within 24 hours of the cleaning. We will re-clean the area at no additional charge.

Chapter 21

USEFUL INFORMATION

Here you will find several useful tips relating to the cleaning industry. Tips to help prevent making mistakes or minimizing the chance of making errors.

*Included in this chapter are the **instructions to log-in** to my website if you have questions that you may have while running residential cleaning business.*

1. Security issues

As in the Real Estate industry, when you are showing properties to a new client, it is wise that you inform someone that you are going to a new address when you are going to a property for the first time. It is important to have a system in place to monitor your whereabouts and your safety.

Have someone check if everything is ok. It is important that before you go to view a residential address for the first time, that someone, be they from your family, friends or coworkers, knows where you are going and check with you that everything is ok. It is also helpful to inform them that all is good when you leave the home.

In my experience you can use something as simple as sending an emoji that is describing your current state. Someone should know what time you have an appointment and connect with you at some point during the visit. Even a text signal can be effective if everything is ok and using a different signal if you are in danger.

2. If you are late

If for some reason you are late, text your client in advance and let them know the exact time that you will now be there. Also, you need to let them know why you are late. Hopefully you will not be later more than 15 minutes, since this may affect your client's plans.

In many cases they hired you as a solution to solve their lack of time and availability to clean their house. Remember you are there to solve their problem and not adding to their time constraints.

Make every effort not to be late at all.

3. Accessing client's homes

Do not lock yourself out of your client's home. Clarify with your client what steps you need to take if something like that should happen. This same information is also useful in case of any emergencies and it is helpful to know whom to call first.

4. Attending local business networking groups

This is a great opportunity to introduce your cleaning business in the area.

5. Receiving bad reviews

If your client gives you a bad review, call them immediately to try and rectify the problem. It is important to be open to any solution that both of you can agree on.

Do everything in your power to remedy this situation to make your client happy.

Then, and only then, ask them to update/edit or remove the negative complaint.

6. Go the extra mile with your clients

Make sure you find out when it is your client's birthday. Set electronic reminders for yourself. Remember them by sending an electronic card or leave a note at their home. It is the little things like this that can make a world of difference for your clients.

It is also a good idea to get innovative about the extras that you can perform randomly for your existing clients. Do things that go above and beyond your scope of work. Every time you are there cleaning, make sure you do something unexpected in addition. Treat this as an appreciation for having them as your client and to be a part of your business. I find it useful to create a list of helpful things I can do for my clients that they will really appreciate.

Questions and Answers

1. Does your client have to sign a contract?

No. Clients will sign a service agreement at the time of their complimentary in-home estimate or via e-mail if it needs to be customized. This service agreement is to acknowledge that you have received their information in writing. There are no terms to this agreement and it may be cancelled at any time giving 48 hours` notice.

2. Who provides cleaning supplies and equipment?

If you have a maid service, you will provide all necessary supplies and equipment to complete the job according to your agreement.

If you have an individual cleaning service or, if this is part your business model you will use your client's supplies and equipment. This is because your goal is to provide customized and sanitary service. Your reason for using their supplies is to make certain that you use them in the exact method they like their home.

In this instance, you also use your client's equipment so that you are sure that there is no cross-contamination with other clients. This stops bacteria and dust from entering your client's house from other homes. This is particularly important for protecting against allergies or bedbugs.

3. How many people should you send for cleaning a client's house?

The good news is that clients can choose how many people they want to clean their home. From time to time, a crew of three may be sent when a person is sick or on vacation and the usual person is unable to come to clean a client's home. You must make every effort to send the same team to your client's home for every clean. This provides consistency and continuity for your clients.

4. What about a key to the house? What if a client is working and will not be there to open the door for you?

If a customer chooses to provide you with a key for entry, please make sure to take every precaution to ensure a client's safety. Client's keys should be stored in a lockbox at your office or safe and should be marked with a code that keeps the client's privacy and security intact.

If a client is not comfortable with providing a key, they also have the option of providing a garage code, a location for a hidden key, or whatever method both of you agree on and are most comfortable with.

5. What if your client has pets?

Make it clear that you love pets! Understand that for many clients, pets are like children. Get to know their names but for security reasons make sure you know how to secure them in one room or area. If your client does have an aggressive pet, ask that they secure them during the cleaning day.

6. Should you service estate cleaning?

Estate cleaning takes place in a residence after a person is deceased. Family may contact you even from out of town or out of state to take care of an estate, either without their participation, or to assist them in this task.

This is most likely a project that requires a lot of time to complete and may take days. It may involve packing family possessions as well as loads of trash removal. After clearing out the area it would be best to perform deep cleaning to prepare the property for sale or alternatively, a move-in.

7. Can your client hire your employee, their service provider directly?

No, they may not. This is a major problem in cleaning industry. A great deal of time and resources are put into hiring and training your staff. Your *Service Agreement* states that your client agrees not to hire any past or present employees for a period of not less than 2 years from the date the employee last worked for your company.

8. For an initial cleaning why is there a higher first-time price?

There are a variety of first time tasks performed during this clean that require extra time and effort. Usually, it requires spending two to three times longer at an initial clean than spent at a regular, recurring clean. This first clean is similar to a "spring clean-up", and is an important part of the first impression you're giving to you're new client. This extra effort will also make subsequent visits less difficult.

9. Why hire maids versus services?

Individual cleaners, or maids, often charge lower weekly rates for house cleaning but this is not always true. Inform your clients that the best option is to interview more than one person and keep an open mind until they have all the details regarding price and the experience of the cleaner.

Residential cleaning services charge more because of the increased costs they face in operating a business – but in the same breath they can also provide more dependability and shoulder the burden of screening and training the individuals coming into your client's home.

10. How to deal with an unhappy client?

Validate all customer concerns through a discussion and invest time in a visit to the client's home. For your next service, call in to see the problem for yourself and make every effort to remedy the situation.

To ask questions go to; <u>https://teresagarvin.com</u>

CONTACT ME - Login with your email and password, ask questions.

In conclusion

As Keith J. Cunningham says,

The goal of business is profitable sustainability, not size. You can't sustain something unless you know what is working and what isn't...and the only way to know for sure is to:

Measure your progress and results.

Identify, correct and improve the activities that are causing those results.

If you want different results, change the activities.

An addiction to big, luck and "hopium" are not strategies.

I have learned a lot from my **great** mentor Anthony Robbins and I would like to share just a tiny portion of it with you:

What is the gap between where you are and where you want to be? Where do you live emotionally? Some people live in anger and disappointment. If you want to change something, work on improving your energy. This will improve your self-esteem and confidence.

People who are wealthy are not lucky they are doing something about it. What's missing in your life? Mostly, time is missing. Don't settle for a life without passion. You need to say I will not be denied! Live a life that is worth living.

What's wrong is always available and so is what's right. You don't have to plant weeds; they grow automatically - just as problems are a sign of life. But again, if you don't have problems, you are not alive. So, aim for a better quality of problems.

Come up with a vision. Every time that you accomplish something, get a new vision and create something that excites you. Most people don't even move. No wonder they are unhappy. The more you move, the more you feel. People expect results instantly, without any work.

Don't be that person!

Focus on what you want. If you didn't have any limits what would your life look like? How would your body look like? What would you do? What would your relationships look like? How about your finances? What extraordinary life would you be living? Wherever your focus goes, energy flows.

Now I want you to do something for yourself. Remember this:

"A DREAM written down with a date becomes a GOAL; a goal broken down into steps becomes a PLAN; a Plan backed by ACTION becomes REALITY"

Take time to think and write about this topic:

If life were extraordinary what would it look like to you - if it were exactly the way you wanted it to be today?

Start with the ultimate end in mind:

1. Life on my terms – how would I make it extraordinary?

2. What would that look like?

3. What would I change, what would I enhance?

4. What would I appreciate more?

5. What would I do?

Do not write a fairytale - just something truly authentic, that will take you from where you are - to where you want to be.

And even if your imagination took you to another form of business it doesn't matter. Cleaning services may not be the desirable business field for you. If it is your chosen field remember that it is only your vehicle to financial independence. Use it to develop your hobbies and have time for your family and construct the social life that you deserve.

Create your Financial Freedom!

Printed in Great Britain
by Amazon

52713131R00088